(5) Debatable	(6) Vote Required	(7) Refer to Rule No.—Page No.		Notes
		17.5	86	
No	Majority	26.2	140	
(a)	Majority	26.3	140	(a) Only as to time and place, not as to date.
No	Majority	26.4	141	
(a)	Majority	26.6	141	
				(b) Demands are not true motions. They have no order of precedence among themselves, and must be disposed of as soon as they arise.
		17.4	86	
No	No vote	15.2	74	
No	No vote	21.2	110	
No	No vote	21.3	110	(c) Also known as parliamentary inquiry.
No	No vote	21.4	111	
No	No vote	21.5	111	(d) Any procedural motion that interferes with discussion requires a $^2/_3$ majority.
No	No vote	21.6	112	
No	No vote	21.7	112	
		17.3	85	
No	2/3 (d)	20.1	101	(e) Only as to date and time for reopening discussion on the main motion.
(e)	2/3	20.2	102	
(e)	2/3	20.3	103	
No	2/3	20.4	103	(f) Only as to the limitations on discussion.
(f)	2/3	20.5	104	
No	2/3	20.6	105	
(g)	2/3	20.7	106	(g) Only as to the terms of reference.
No	Majority	9.1	37	(h) Only as to the scope of the subject and the selection of Chair.
No	Majority	9.2	39	
(i)	(k)	18.1	91	(i) Only as to the amendment.
(j)	(k)	18.3	95	
(l)	(k)	17.9	88	(j) Only as to the sub-amendment.
Yes	(k) (m)	17.10	89	
Yes	(k)	25.1	135	(k) Requires the same majority as does the main motion or resolution to which it refers.
Yes	(k)	25.2	135	
Yes	(k)	25.3	136	(l) Only as to the wisdom of dividing.
No	Unanimous	25.4	137	
				(m) A motion may be informally withdrawn by the mover before it has been seconded or stated by the Chair.
Yes	(n)	17.2	85	
No	—	24.1	127	(n) Simple majority unless a higher majority is required by the constitution.
No	Majority	24.2	128	
No	Majority	24.6	132	
No	Majority	24.7	133	

Wainberg's Society Meetings
Including Rules of Order

J.M. Wainberg, Q.C.
Mark I. Wainberg, B.A., LL.B.

CCH CANADIAN LIMITED

TAX AND BUSINESS LAW PUBLISHERS

HEAD OFFICE: 6 GARAMOND CT., DON MILLS, ONT. M3C 1Z5.
TELEPHONE (416) 441-2992. FAX NO. (416) 444-9011.

MONTREAL, PQ	OTTAWA, ON	TORONTO, ON	KITCHENER, ON	CALGARY, AB	VANCOUVER, BC
(514) 866-2771	(613) 235-8414	(416) 250-0860	(519) 741-8442	(403) 269-2169	(604) 688-7510

4003

Published by CCH Canadian Limited

USA	Commerce Clearing House Inc., Riverwoods, Illinois.
UK and EUROPE	CCH Editions Limited, Bicester, Oxfordshire.
AUSTRALIA	CCH Australia Limited, North Ryde, NSW.
NEW ZEALAND	CCH New Zealand Limited, Auckland.
SINGAPORE, MALAYSIA and BRUNEI	CCH Asia Limited, Singapore.
JAPAN	CCH Japan Limited, Tokyo.

Important Disclaimer: This publication is sold with the understanding that (1) the authors and editors are not responsible for the results of any actions taken on the basis of information in this work, nor for any errors or omissions; and (2) the publisher is not engaged in rendering legal, accounting or other professional services. The publisher, and the authors and editors, expressly disclaim all and any liability to any person, whether a purchaser of this publication or not, in respect of anything and of the consequences of anything done or omitted to be done by any such person in reliance, whether whole or partial, upon the whole or any part of the contents of this publication. If legal advice or other expert assistance is required, the services of a competent professional person should be sought.

Ownership of Trade Marks

CCH ACCESS, COMPUTAX and **COMMERCE CLEARING HOUSE, INC.**

are the property of Commerce Clearing House Incorporated, Riverwoods, Illinois, U.S.A.

Canadian Cataloguing in Publication Data

```
Wainberg, J. M., 1906-
   Wainberg's society meetings including rules
of order

Includes index.
ISBN 0-88796-569-5

1. Parliamentary practice - Canada.  I. Wainberg,
Mark I.  II. Title.

JF515.W35 1991        060.4'2      C92-093175-8
```

© **1992, Wainlex Limited**

Typeset and printed in Canada by CCH Canadian Limited.

PREFACE

Company meetings in Canada are conducted according to procedures laid down by precedent and common law emanating from British parliamentary practice. On the whole, statutes are silent as to the conduct of meetings, and bylaws have as many versions as there are lawyers.

For the backbone of the original text of "Company Meetings" I had to draw primarily on my own experience in the conduct of meetings and in proxy fights for control of companies, as well as from ensuing litigation.

For "Society Meetings", even more than for "Company Meetings", I gratefully acknowledge the assistance of my son and full-fledged co-author, Mark Wainberg (B.A., LL.B., University of Toronto), whose considerable experience as a lawyer, writer, editor, and member of numerous non-profit organizations has been invaluable in the preparation of this work.

We both acknowledge the contributions of my daughters, Sandra Cytrynbaum (B.A. Hon. and Teacher's Certificate, University of Toronto), who has had extensive experience in social, musical and charitable organizations, and Ruth Lowenberg (B.Sc., University of Toronto and M.S., Cornell University), who has been active in scientific, nutrition and dietary organizations. They have each attended and chaired numerous meetings.

The authors would like to hear from readers with suggestions that would make the book even more helpful.

J. M. Wainberg

Toronto
August 1992

INTRODUCTION

The function of rules of order is to maintain decorum and ascertain the will of the majority while preserving the rights of the minority.

It is not claimed that all the rules contained in this work have specific statutory authority. These rules are based partly upon common law, and partly upon British parliamentary procedure, as varied by accepted usage. In a few instances, where a hiatus appeared to exist, a rule has been enunciated in the spirit of the democratic rights, which are intended to be preserved by parliamentary rules of order.

When the majority decision has been determined by a vote, that vote becomes the decision of the assembly. It is then the duty of the minority to accept and abide by the decision. This is the unwritten law in a democracy. When a member joins the group, he tacitly agrees to be governed by the majority, provided that the majority does not oppress the minority.

The rights of the minority are protected by the quorum rule, the right to be heard, the right to enter into the discussion on any motion, the right to make a motion and have it considered, and the right to expect that the governing statute, the constitution, and the rules of order will be followed.

This work applies to all incorporated and unincorporated organizations without share capital, and to some organizations with share capital where the "one person–one vote" rule applies.

It makes no pretense of being an academic treatise; rather, it is intended as a manual, to be referred to during the course of a meeting for quick, ready answers. The index has been designed with this in mind; it is highly cross-referenced and detailed. While most indices give a list of page numbers on which the subject can be found, the index in this book (and all others written by these authors) gives the exact location of the subject sought without having to flip through page after page. The time saved and the convenience is welcomed by all readers.

Included in this work is a chapter on Condominiums written in consultation with Jonathan Fine, B.Sc., LL.B., and a chapter on Co-operatives and Credit Unions by Garry Gillam, LL.B. Each author is a leader in his field, and their expertise in these areas has been a valuable contribution.

A word of caution: the practice relating to the conduct of either company or society meetings is not the same on all points in Canada and the U.S.A., or even in England or Australia.

Although all the procedures and rules derive from the Mother of Parliaments, each child has developed differently. Some genes have survived, others have mutated to reflect the times and the people.

Authors of parliamentary procedure books seldom agree on all rules. We have selected the versions most common in Canada that follow the basic rule set out in the first paragraph above. In many of the rules we are supported by the Rules of Procedure in the Standing Orders of the House of Commons. In others, we have relied on our practical experience spanning six decades.

J. M. Wainberg

Mark Wainberg

TABLE OF CONTENTS

GLOSSARY

Abstain (Abstention)
> To refrain from voting.

Ad hoc committee
> _See "Special committee"._

Adopt
> Agree to be bound by and to comply with. To adopt a report is to concur with its recommendations and agree to implement them. Rules of order (such as Wainberg's) and reports are adopted.

> Approve. To give consent. To consent to a past or future act or expenditure. To agree with the content of a document, e.g., financial statements, budgets, agendas, etc.

> Confirm. To approve. To ratify. Certain bylaws and resolutions must be confirmed by the members before becoming effective.

> Ratify. To confirm or make valid by formal consent. To approve of an act after it has been done, or to approve of an agreement after it has been executed. Corporate acts are ratified.

> Verify. To authenticate as true or correct. Minutes can be verified only by members who were present. Verifying does not imply adopting.

> _Note: These words are collected under one heading because they are often misunderstood and misused._

Adjourn
> To defer to another day. An adjournment may or may not be to a fixed day. If all the business for which the meeting was called has been dealt with, the meeting should be "concluded". (_See "Concluding Meeting", Rule 26.2, page 140, "Recessing Meeting", Rule 26.6, page 141, and "Adjourning Meeting to Fixed Date/Without Fixed Date", Rules 26.3 and 26.4, pages 140–141.)_

Adjourned meeting
> _See "Reconvened meeting". (See also Rule 26.8, page 142.)_

Agenda
> A list of things to be done; the order of business to be brought up, discussed, and disposed of.

Amend
> To change by adding, deleting, or substituting words. Not all motions are amendable. (_See chart, inside front cover._)

Amendment
> A motion to vary the motion under discussion.

Announcement
> *See "Declaration".*

Apply
> A motion "applies" to or has an effect on another motion when it alters, affects, or disposes of the original motion.

Appointment
> The act of naming for an office (*see Rule 24.7, page 133*). No choice is implied. (*See "Election".*)

Appointor
> A person or entity who appoints a proxyholder or an agent. (*See "Proxyholder".*)

Approve
> *See "Adopt".*

Association
> A society or societies made up of persons who are united together by mutual consent in order to deliberate, determine, and act jointly for a common purpose other than the acquisition of gain. (*See also ¶ 100, page 3.*)

Ballot
> A paper (either printed or blank) on which the voter records his vote.

Bylaw
> (Omitting the hyphen is the modern trend and is supported by good authority.) A permanent, continuing rule to be applied to future occasions, in contrast to a resolution, which applies only to a single act of a society. (*See also "Special bylaw".*)

Call to order, come to order
> A request by the Chair at the beginning of a meeting, assuming his authority and requesting everyone's attention.

Casting vote
> A second vote by the Chair, exercisable in addition to his own vote as a director or member, and permissible only if specifically granted by the constitution.

Chair
> The person who conducts the meeting, the presiding officer. The Chair always refers to himself/herself and is referred to as the "Chair". Chair is intended to cover both genders.

Chairman, Chairwoman, Chairperson
> *See "Chair".*

Club

A society made up of a group of persons who are associated for the promotion of politics, sport, art, science, or literature, or for any purpose other than the acquisition of gain. (*See also ¶ 100, page 3.*)

Committee

A group of members or directors to whom a matter is referred for deliberation, study, action, or recommendation. A committee may be discharged at any time by the authority which appointed it.

Common law

Law based upon court decisions and general custom.

Conclude

To bring to a close after completion of all business.

Confirm

See "Adopt".

Consideration, objecting to

See "Objecting to consideration".

Constitution

The document or documents creating the society. Most constitutions also provide machinery by which the society carries on its operations and dissolves. (*See Chapter 2, Constitution, page 9.*)

Convene

To formally open a meeting.

Cum die

To a fixed day. (*See "Adjourn".*)

Debate

Discussion; an open argument for or against a motion.

Declaration

A decision of the Chair. (*See Rule 10.2, page 44.*)

De facto directors

Persons not duly elected as directors who act as directors.

Demand

A request made to the Chair for his/her action. (*See Chapter 21, page 109, and chart, inside front cover.*)

Election

The act of choosing or selecting one or more from a number of people; making a choice by any manifestation of preference. "Appointing", however, is merely the act of naming a person to hold an official position in the society. (*See Rules 24.1–24.6, pages 127–132. See also "Appointment".*)

Ex officio

See Rule 8.4(iii), page 34. The constitution may provide that a person holding an official position in the community or in another society may be appointed an *ex officio* director, officer, or member of a society. This may include current or former members or officers of the society.

Expunge

To delete or obliterate a resolution or comment from the minutes.

Floor

The right to speak. The person who "has the floor" has the right to speak and no one else may speak, except in strict accordance with the rules, until the Chair gives the floor to another. A subject on the floor (on the table) is a subject before the meeting. *See "Lay on the table".*

Germane

Pertaining or relating directly to the subject.

Information, point of

See "Point of information".

Inquiry

See "Point of procedure".

Lay on the table

To postpone discussion on a matter. At one time Canadian societies accepted and followed the English meaning, "to open temporarily for discussion". However, the U.S. influence has been so strong that "lay on the table", or "to lay on the table temporarily", is now accepted by some to mean "postpone". In order to avoid confusion, words should be added to remove any doubts or ambiguities, e.g., "to lay on the table and postpone", or "to lay on the table until a member revives it on a motion", or words to that effect. (*See also "Shelve".*)

Main motion

A proposal put to the meeting for discussion and decision. (*See "Motion".*) (*See also chart, inside front cover.*)

Majority

The percentage of votes required to pass a motion. (*See also "Simple majority", "Resolution", and "Special resolution".*)

Meeting

The coming together of two or more persons with the common intention of transacting business. A session is part of a meeting. (*See also "Session".*)

Minority

Less than half of the votes cast, less than half of the members present at a meeting, or less than half of the total membership, depending on the constitution. (*See also "Majority".*)

Minutes

The official record of a meeting or a session.

Motion

A proposal to do something, to order something to be done, or to express an opinion about something. The subject-matter of the motion is called a "question". A motion, when duly passed, becomes a "resolution".

Nominate

To propose someone to an office to be filled. (*See Rule 24.1, page 127.*)

Objecting to consideration

A motion to drop the subject. A motion objecting to the consideration of the motion being discussed must be made while the subject is under discussion and before it is seconded. (*See Rule 20.1, page 101.*)

Order of the day

An old parliamentary device that fixes a specific time for the consideration of a subject in order to assure the greatest possible attendance of interested members.

Out of order

Contrary to parliamentary procedure or *ultra vires*. Irrelevant. Not germane.

Parliamentary inquiry

See "Point of procedure".

Point of information

Asking the Chair to clarify or explain the content or background of a motion. (*See Rule 21.4, page 111.*)

Point of order

A request to correct a situation which violates a rule of parliamentary procedure. (*See Rule 21.6, page 112.*)

Point of (personal) privilege

See "Privilege".

Point of procedure

A request for information on the proper procedure to be followed at a meeting.

Poll
> A common law method of voting, in which each voter, by his personal act, delivers his vote to the Chair, or answers a roll call.

Postpone
> To defer a discussion which has not commenced. (*See also "Adjourn".*)

Precedence
> The right of way of one motion over another. (*See chart, inside front cover, for order of precedence of motions.*)

Presiding officer
> See "Chair".

Previous question
> Archaic form (not used currently) of "putting the question" (*see below*).

Privilege
> The right to immediate consideration (without a seconder) of a matter which affects the meeting or any individual thereof regarding safety, orderliness, comfort, or reputation.

Privileged motion
> A motion having a high priority. A motion to conclude, terminate, or adjourn has the highest priority.

Procedural motion
> A motion dealing with procedure as distinguished from a substantive motion.

Proposition
> A suggestion not yet formally phrased as a motion or a resolution. The Chair may sometimes permit a general conversation around a subject with the intent that a resolution or a motion will evolve therefrom.

Proxy
> A signed power of attorney authorizing someone to act on behalf of a member at a meeting. (*See "Proxyholder".*)

Proxyform
> An unsigned proxy.

Proxyholder
> The agent or attorney appointed by and for a member. (*See also "Proxy".*)

Putting the question
> A motion to close discussion, terminate debate, or vote immediately.

Question

The subject-matter of a motion. To call a "question" is a call for a vote on the motion. Use the word "vote" instead.

Quorum

The minimum number of qualified persons whose presence at a meeting is requisite in order that business may be legally transacted.

Rank

See "Precedence".

Ratify

To confirm or make valid by formal consent in writing. To approve of an act after it has been done, or to approve of an agreement after it has been executed.

Recess

A short interruption of a meeting or a session of a meeting. This is shorter than an adjournment. Recess is usually a matter of minutes or a few hours at most, for the purpose of relaxation, lunch, settlement of disputes between factions, or the counting of ballots. (*See Rule 26.6, page 141.*)

Recognize

The Chair "recognizes" the member, thereby giving him/her the floor and the right to speak. (*See "Floor".*)

Reconsider

To open up and to review a matter previously disposed of, for the purpose of voting on it again.

Reconvened meeting

The continuation of a meeting which had been adjourned.

Repeal

See "Rescind".

Rescind

To cancel, quash, void, or nullify a resolution.

Resolution

The result of a motion that has been passed.

Rules of order

The rules that govern procedures and rights of members at meetings of members, boards, and committees as in *Wainberg's Society Meetings* and *Wainberg's Company Meetings.*

Scrutineer

A clerk or teller appointed by the Chair or by the meeting to assist the Chair in counting attendance, collecting, examining, and tabulating the proxies and ballots, and in determining the vote.

Seconding a motion

To consent to a motion being discussed by the meeting. Seconding does not necessarily approve of the motion itself, nor does it obligate the seconder to vote in favour of it.

Sense of the meeting

The opinion, decision, or feeling of those present; the "sense of the meeting" need not be unanimous.

Session

A sitting or a part of a meeting. It may be the portion of the meeting which is held before noon, or that which is held in the afternoon, both of which together constitute a meeting. (*See also "Meeting".*)

Shelve

To suspend or put away any further consideration of a matter.

Show of hands

An informal method of voting which eliminates the necessity of taking a poll, unless a poll is demanded. (*See Rule 22.5, page 117.*)

Silent assent

Acquiescence; assumption of general concurrence based on the fact that no objection is voiced. (*See Rule 22.4, page 117.*)

Simple majority

More than half (of the votes cast, of those present at a meeting, or of the total membership, depending on the constitution).

Sine die

With no fixed date. (*See "Adjourn".*)

Sitting

See "Session".

Society

An association; a club. (*See "Association", "Club".*)

Special bylaw

A bylaw requiring confirmation by more than a simple majority (usually two-thirds of the members). (*See "Bylaw".*)

Special committee, *ad hoc* committee

A committee set up for a specific purpose.

Special order

A parliamentary device that fixes a specific time in the near future to consider a motion or subject, giving it an absolute priority at that time. (*See Rule 13.6, page 68.*)

Special resolution
A resolution requiring more than a simple majority, usually two-thirds. (*See "Resolution".*)

Stating the question
Before calling for a vote, the Chair restates the motion, clarifying it at the same time if necessary.

Sub-amendment
An amendment to an amendment.

Substantive motion
A main motion. A motion proposing a concrete matter of business as distinguished from a procedural motion.

Table
See *"Lay on the table".*

Terminate
See *"Conclude".*

Unanimous vote
With no dissenting vote, but possible abstentions.

Unfinished business
Any business left over from a previous meeting, either by the adjournment of the previous meeting, or by a specific motion to postpone a matter to a subsequent meeting.

Verify
See *"Adopt".*

Yield
A motion yields to another if that other has a higher precedence or rank. The speaker having the floor may yield the floor to another member of his own volition, or at the request of the Chair. (*See also "Precedence".*)

PART I

STRUCTURE

CHAPTER 1

Societies

¶ 100   Introduction

A "society" is an organization consisting of people

(a) who have come together for a common purpose or to pursue common activities of a patriotic, religious, philanthropic, social, professional, fraternal, sporting, athletic, or other non-business nature, and

(b) who carry on their common purpose or pursue their common activities under a name which is different from the names of the individual members.

In this work, "society" includes a club or association (in some jurisdictions, "association" means a combination of societies or clubs).

A society may be incorporated or unincorporated, and, if incorporated, may or may not have share capital. A society is to be distinguished from a "business". The main purpose of a business is the pursuit of profit, whereas in a society, profit is either irrelevant or merely ancillary to the common purpose or common activities. However, the members of a society may help each other make money for themselves as individuals. For example, professional societies often conduct seminars in order to improve the skills and increase the earning power of the individual members.

¶ 105   Organization Models

There are two basic models for organization of societies: the direct and the indirect, with dozens of variations and combinations to suit individual circumstances.

(i) *Direct (Member-Centred) Model*

In the direct model of organization, the members (who may be persons, corporations, societies, or countries) elect the president and the Chair as well as other officers and directors. All of these officials have a direct connection with the members, and they rely on the members to keep them in office and to re-elect them.

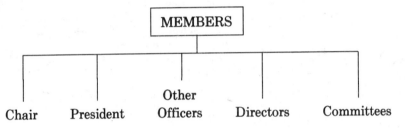

(ii) *Indirect (Board-Centred) Model*

In the indirect model of organization, the members elect the directors, and the board elects or appoints the Chair, the president, and the other officers. These officials rely mainly on the board to keep them in office and to re-elect them. They usually have a stronger loyalty to the directors than to the members.

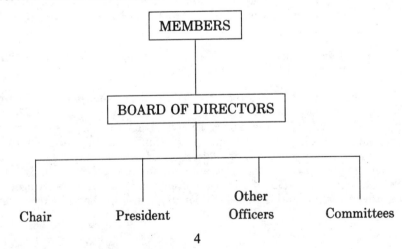

4

(iii) *Hybrid Model*

Variations of the two basic models frequently occur in multi-tiered national organizations. The "pure" direct model tends to be unworkable in national organizations. A hybrid direct/indirect model is often used, whereby the delegates at national meetings or conventions elect the national officers and the directors, and the board then elects the executive committee. Another hybrid uses the indirect model at the national level (whereby the national meetings elect the directors to the board which in turn elects the national officers and the executive committee), and the direct model at the local level.

¶110 Unincorporated Societies

Any number of persons or corporations or other entities may organize themselves into a society (club, association, etc.) without the benefit of incorporation.

¶115 Disadvantages

There are several disadvantages of unincorporated societies:

(i) *Liability for Debts of the Society*

Members, including officials and other persons acting on behalf of the society, may be personally liable for debts.

The personal liability of a member of an unincorporated society for debts of the society depends upon the circumstances. The legal principles of agency usually prevail. If the member who is incurring the debt has actual authority from the other members to do so, or if the other members maintain that this member is authorized to incur the debt, or if the other members ratify the transaction, then an agency relationship exists; thus the member incurring the debt is deemed to be an agent for the members, who are then personally liable for the debt. If no agency relationship can be established, the contracting party is personally liable for the debt.

(ii) *Liability for Torts of Others*

Members of unincorporated societies, including officials and other persons acting on behalf of the society, may be personally liable for torts (negligence, etc.) of others.

A tort is a civil wrong other than a breach of contract. The liability in tort of a member of an unincorporated society for wrongful acts or omissions of others acting on his behalf (agents, trustees, officers, or servants) depends upon the position of the wrongdoer. For example, if the wrongdoer was acting within the scope of his express or implied authority, or within the course of his employment, or with the knowledge of the members, then the members may be personally liable for the torts of the wrongdoer.

(iii) *No Legal Entity*

Since an unincorporated society has no legal existence, it cannot enter into contracts in its own name, nor can it sue in its own name.

(iv) *No Property*

An unincorporated society cannot own or lease real or personal property in its own name. When an unincorporated body (other than a partnership) wishes to hold property, the property must be held in the name of trustees. The terms of the trust should be set out in a formal trust agreement.

(v) *Distribution of Assets*

Upon dissolution of the society, there may be difficulty in dealing with its assets, unless there is a formal trust agreement.

¶ 120 Incorporated Societies

(i) *Incorporation*

All legislatures in Canada have enacted statutes to incorporate corporations with share capital and corporations without share capital.

If the objects of the society come within federal jurisdiction, incorporation under a federal statute is appropriate. If the society is local in nature or confined to a particular province, incorporation under a provincial statute is appropriate. Such a society may be permitted to carry on its objects out of the province under the extra-provincial provisions of the provincial acts.

(ii) *Capital (Financing)*

Incorporated societies finance themselves through membership entrance fees, annual dues, levies, and donations, as well as through entrepreneurial projects such as athletic and sporting events, sales of articles and goods, bingos, lotteries, and other projects. Such societies may also rely on donations and grants from governments and foundations. They may also finance themselves by borrowing, since they have the capacity to execute promissory notes, land mortgages, chattel mortgages, and debentures. Incorporated societies with share capital also finance themselves through the sale of shares.

(iii) *Personal Liability*

A member of an incorporated society (except a member of a condominium corporation (*see Chapter 31, Condominium Corporations, page 165*)) is not liable as such for the debts or torts of the society; however, if the member is also a director, he may be personally liable to creditors in cases of negligence or breach of duty.

(iv) *Legal Capacity*

- incorporated societies may enter into contracts and leases
- incorporated societies may sue and be sued in the societies' names

(v) *"Non-Profit" Incorporated Societies*

Some provincial statutes require that non-share capital societies incorporated under those statutes be "non-profit" societies, that is, that they comply with the following guidelines:

(a) the society shall operate without purpose of gain for its members;

(b) all profits and other gains shall be used in promoting its objects;

(c) the directors shall serve as such without remuneration, and shall not, directly or indirectly, receive any profits apart from being paid their reasonable expenses;

(d) upon dissolution, after payment of all debts and liabilities, the remaining property shall be distributed to another society with similar objects, or to a charity.

¶ 125 Societies With Share Capital

- members are not liable for debts or torts of the society (except in the case of unpaid subscriptions)
- societies may enter into contracts and leases
- societies may sue and be sued in the societies' names

CHAPTER 2

The Constitution

¶ 200   Introduction

Every organization, whether incorporated or not, should have a constitution. The constitution should declare the existence of the organization and also provide machinery by which the society carries on and dissolves.

¶ 205   Elements of the Constitution

Incorporated Society: If the society is incorporated, the constitution includes (1) the governing statute, (2) the incorporating document which creates the organization (letters patent, memorandum, or articles of association or incorporation issued by the government), together with (3) the bylaws of the society.

Unincorporated Society: If the society is not incorporated, the document should set out the purposes or objectives of the organization, the distribution of powers (members, board of directors, officers and committees), criteria for membership, and procedures to amend the constitution, together with the bylaws (sometimes called "rules", "regulations", or "procedures").

The constitution should be in writing and signed by the required number of members according to its own regulation.

9

¶ 210   Summary of the Constitution

Some incorporated societies issue a document entitled "Constitution" which may contain all or some of the following:

- the aims and objectives of the society;

- distribution of powers among the members, committees, etc.;

- parts of the statute under which the society was incorporated that may affect the day-to-day operations of the society;

- the charter, letters patent, or memorandum or articles of association or incorporation; and

- the bylaws, including procedures for amending the bylaws.

¶ 215   Distribution to Members

Every member is entitled to receive a copy of the constitution (*see* ¶ 205). Societies sometimes distribute a document (improperly referred to as "the constitution") which may be a summary of part of the constitution or unofficial additions to it.

CHAPTER 3

Bylaws

¶300 Introduction

The bylaws establish the procedures under which the society carries out its objects. They are considered part of the constitution (*see Chapter 2, The Constitution, page 9*) and are more easily changed than the incorporating documents (articles, letters patents, special acts). To amend the objects or any other item in the incorporating documents, it is necessary to go back to the government department that issued the incorporating document.

¶305 Contents of Bylaws

The bylaws may cover the following items:

- membership qualifications, limits on numbers, classes of membership, resignations, expulsion of members, *ex officio* members;

- board of directors: number, election, removal, remuneration, *ex officio* directors;

- board meetings: notice, quorum, minutes;

- officers: duties, election, removal, remuneration, *ex officio;*

- committees: executive committee, other standing committees, special (*ad hoc*) committees, committee members;

- members' meetings: procedures for calling and conducting meetings, annual meetings, regular meetings, special meetings, notice requirements, etc., chairing the meeting, quorum; minutes;

- indemnities to directors, officers, and others;

11

- execution of documents;
- voting, voting methods, majorities required;
- proxies (if permitted), proxy solicitation;
- banking, auditors, financial year, books and records, custody of books and records;
- fees, dues, assessments;
- procedures for amendment of bylaws;
- rules and regulations;
- adoption of rules of order (*see ¶ 320, below*).

¶ 310 Filing of Bylaws (*Canada Corporations Act*)

To obtain a federal letters patent, a copy of the proposed bylaws must be filed with the application. For this purpose, the Corporations Branch of the Department of Consumer and Corporate Affairs, Canada, issues sample bylaws. While the suggestions are not rigid, certain points must be covered. Other points are optional as long as they do not conflict with any provision of the law.

¶ 315 Entrenchment of Bylaws

In all jurisdictions, provisions which could be included in the bylaws may be included in the incorporating document. Such provisions are then more deeply entrenched and more complicated to change. The governing acts set out the procedure for changing the incorporating document.

¶ 320 Adoption of Rules of Order

To adopt these rules of order, the following should be included or added to the bylaws:

"The Society adopts and declares that *Wainberg's Society Meetings including Rules of Order* (latest edition) shall govern the affairs of the Society and the conduct of all meetings, provided that any of the rules therein may be altered by an amending bylaw passed in accordance with the constitution."

CHAPTER 4

Voting Systems

¶ 400   Introduction

The bylaws of the society will set out the voting systems which apply to it, as well as the voting methods (*see Chapter 22, Voting Methods, page 115*).

Whatever method of voting is used, the minority is bound by the decision of the majority, provided that (a) the meeting was duly convened, (b) the vote was duly conducted, and (c) the motion was passed with the required majority, or in the case of election, the persons declared elected received the highest numbers of votes.

¶ 405   Systems of Voting

The most common voting systems are:

(i) *Basic* (selecting one from two or more alternatives — persons or options)

The voter has the choice of voting for one of the alternatives or not voting at all (abstaining).

(ii) *Basic Plus* (selecting two from three or more alternatives)

The voter has the choice of two votes, one vote, or abstaining from voting. (In some societies, the constitution does not permit fewer than the required number to be elected or selected.)

(iii) *Cumulative*

The voter has the number of votes equal to the number of vacancies to be filled or options to be selected. He may use all of them in favour of one or more of the choices available, but the total must not exceed the number of vacancies to be filled or options to be selected.

(iv) *Ranking*

The voter indicates on the ballot his order of preference, e.g., 1, 2, 3, etc. The numbers in favour of each choice are tabulated, and the choice with the *lowest* number prevails. (If there are more than two vacancies to be filled, the choice of the two lowest numbers prevails.) If the voter does not give a ranking to each choice, his vote is wasted.

The specific ways in which these systems are applied are set out in Chapter 22, Voting Methods, page 115.

CHAPTER 5

Members

¶ 500   Introduction

Members are accepted into a society because (a) they sympathize with its aims and purposes, (b) they qualify or conform to its tenets, and (c) they agree tacitly or in writing to comply with its constitution.

Rule 5.1   Members

Every person who joins a group (whether incorporated or not) is bound by the constitution or practices of the group and to any changes properly made in the constitution or practices.

Rule 5.2   Membership

Memberships may be made transferable or non-transferable by the constitution. If the memberships are made specifically transferable by the constitution, no bylaw can restrict transfers.

Rule 5.3   Classes of Membership

Memberships may be divided into various classes according to the nature of the society. There is no uniformity in the designations or in the number of classes in each society. The classes are defined in the constitution, usually in the bylaws.

The following are some of the typical classes of memberships found in constitutions:

(i) *Regular Members*

- participate fully in the activities of the society

(ii) *Intermediate Members*

- may be in a certain age frame, e.g., junior, senior

(iii) *Honorary/Ex Officio Members*[1]

- honorary members are usually appointed by the board
- are exempt from paying membership dues
- cannot hold office but may enjoy all other rights and privileges of membership
- may be retired professionals in a professional society, for example
- *ex officio* members are admitted into the society by virtue of their positions as office-holders in another society or governmental body

(iv) *Life Members*

- are appointed for life in recognition of past service to the society, or upon payment of a specified financial contribution

(v) *Honorary Life Members*

- hold both life and honorary membership status

(vi) *Affiliate Members*

- are interested in the purposes of the society but may not be fully qualified to join as active members, e.g., non-professional spouses of members of a professional society, members who live outside the area

(vii) *Associate Members*

- could be female members in a men's club or male members in a women's club, or members who live outside the area
- usually have all the rights of members except the right to vote or hold office

---

[1] *See also Rule 6.6, Honorary/Ex Officio Directors, page 20.*

Rule 5.4   Expulsion

Expulsion is the permanent removal of all privileges of membership (*see also Rule 5.5, Suspension*). Expulsion must be done in accordance with the constitution of the society and the rules of natural justice. There must be "fair play". The member must have notice of the reason for his proposed expulsion, and a reasonable opportunity to be heard by the body which makes the decision.

(i) *Non-Payment of Dues*

A member who is in arrears in the payment of dues is not automatically deprived of his status as a member in good standing, unless the rules of the society so provide.

Although a society may purport to expel a member for non-payment of dues, the courts, despite their reluctance to interfere with the internal workings of the society, will inquire as to the true motives which induced the expulsion. If the expulsion is not bona fide, or if there has been a failure of natural justice (e.g., if the member has not been given an opportunity to be heard), the member will be reinstated by the courts.

(ii) *Cause*

A member can be expelled for cause only if

(a) the constitution (bylaws or rules) provides in plain and unambiguous language that the society has the power to expel;

(b) the decision is made bona fide;

(c) the decision to expel is based upon a specific act of the member which is inconsistent with the aims, objects, and ethics of the society;

(d) the member is given an opportunity to defend himself after adequate advance notice, and is given a warning of the consequences if he fails to attend the hearing;

(e) the procedures followed are in conformity with the constitution and in accordance with natural justice.

While the courts are usually reluctant to interfere in the internal operation of a society, they are more apt to intervene in the case of an expulsion from the society, especially if the society owns property.

(iii) *Damages*

A wrongful expulsion may give rise to a claim for monetary damages. *See Chapter 28, Ejection from Meetings, page 149.*

Rule 5.5 Suspension

Suspension is the temporary removal of the privileges of membership (*see also Rule 5.4, Expulsion*). If a member violates any of the written rules of society, but such violation is not a sufficient ground for expulsion, he may be suspended. If a member is suspended, some or all of his privileges may be removed until he corrects the violation or default, or until he begins to observe the rule.

If the violation is of a serious nature (according to the rules of the society), or if the suspended member refuses or neglects to correct the default or observe a rule for which he was suspended, he may be expelled (*see Rule 5.4, Expulsion*).

CHAPTER 6

Directors

Rule 6.1 Board of Directors

The affairs of the society are managed by its board of directors (sometimes called Board of Regents or Board of Governors). The constitution or bylaws establish the method of election of the directors, which varies according to the nature of the organization. (*See ¶ 105, Organization Models, page 4.*)

Rule 6.2 Number of Directors

Some acts and constitutions provide for a minimum number of directors on a board, whereas others provide for a minimum and a maximum number of directors.

Rule 6.3 Term of Office

Some constitutions provide for a fixed term of one or two years, while others provide for terms of up to three years, rotating every year.

Rule 6.4 Qualification

Every director must be over eighteen years of age and must not be an undischarged bankrupt. In most cases, directors must be members of the organization. Notable exceptions are hospitals and stock exchanges, in which the directors of the board are not necessarily members of the institution. Several condominium statutes allow non-owners to be directors.

Rule 6.5   Liability

Directors of societies must be honest, loyal, careful, and diligent. A director, as well as an officer, must disclose to the society any interest, direct or indirect, that he has in a contract or proposed contract between the society and another society, corporation, or person. A director will be held accountable for any profits or gains realized from a contract or transaction in which he is interested unless he:

- declared and disclosed his interest at a meeting of the society or the board;

- did not vote as a director in respect thereof; and

- acted honestly and in good faith at the time.

Directors also have numerous liabilities (civil, criminal, and administrative) and rights under various statutes (e.g., for employees' wages). There is insurance available for the protection of officers and directors.

See also Wainberg's Duties and Responsibilities of Directors in Canada.[1]

Rule 6.6   Honorary/Ex Officio Directors

The constitution of the society may provide that a person not otherwise qualified may be appointed an honorary or *ex officio* director[2] if he has formerly been a director or officer of the society, or if he has held a specified office in some other government/non-government organization.

Rule 6.7   Attendance at Meetings

Only directors may attend, participate in, and vote at board meetings. Other persons, including members, may attend only at the pleasure of the board, as a privilege, not as a right.

Ex officio directors have the right to attend meetings and participate in discussions, but do not have the right to vote unless the constitution specifically allows them to do so.

Voting by proxy or ballots is not permitted at board meetings unless the constitution specifically permits it.

---

[1] J.M. Wainberg and M.I. Wainberg, *Duties and Responsibilities of Directors in Canada*, 6th ed. (Toronto: CCH Canadian Limited, 1987).

[2] *See also Rule 5.3(iii), Honorary/Ex Officio Members, page 16.*

Rule 6.8 Vacancies on the Board

In the case of a vacancy, and as long as a quorum remains in office, the board may continue to function. Unless the constitution permits the board to appoint a qualified person to fill the vacancy, the members must fill the vacancy at a general meeting.

Even if the constitution permits the board to fill a vacancy, it cannot fill the vacancy when (a) there is no quorum in existence, (b) the vacancy arises from the removal of a director by the members, or (c) the vacancy arises from an increase in the number of directors. In these cases, the remaining members of the board are obligated to immediately call a meeting of members in order to fill the vacancy.

Rule 6.9 Removal of Directors

Subject to provisions to the contrary in the constitution, a director may be removed from office by the members at any time before the expiration of his term, with or without cause. Even if the appointment is for the ensuing year or until his successor is appointed, no vested right is conferred on the director to hold his office for any length of time. The prescribed procedures must be strictly adhered to.

Before proceeding with a motion to remove, it is prudent to advise the director of the intention to remove him, and to give him the opportunity to resign.

(i) *Motion*

"That A.B. be removed as a director, effective immediately." (The reasons for his removal may be added.)

(ii) *Characteristics*

A motion to remove a director is a main motion (*see chart, inside front cover*) that

- requires seconding;

- is amendable as to effective date and recitals; and

- requires a simple majority.

The director must be given reasonable notice of the motion and of the meeting at which the motion is to be considered.

21

(iii) *Notice of Removal*

The notice must include

- the date, time, and place of the meeting;
- the proposed motion for removal, or a summary of the motion;
- the nature of the alleged misconduct, if misconduct is being alleged;
- a statement advising the director that he may attend the meeting with his counsel, and make submissions in his defence; and
- a statement informing the director that, if he does not attend, the meeting may proceed in his absence and he will not be entitled to any further notice.

(iv) *Rights at Meeting*

The director is entitled to attend the meeting, speak on his own behalf, be represented by counsel or an agent, bring in documentary evidence (witnesses' statements, etc.), and hear all complaints against him. He is also entitled to make the final statement after everyone has spoken and immediately before the vote is taken.

(v) *Requisitioned Meeting to Remove Directors*

Some statutes governing incorporated societies authorize a small percentage of the members to requisition the calling of a general meeting to pass any motion that is connected with the affairs of the society and that is not inconsistent with the governing statute. This would include a motion to remove directors. (*See also ¶ 2920, Requisitioned Meetings, Motions, and Circulated Statements, page 158.*)

Rule 6.10   Conflict of Interest

A conflict of interest may arise in situations:

(a) where a director makes a decision or does an act motivated by other or additional considerations than the "best interests of the society" ("collateral purpose");

(b) where a director personally contracts with his society or where he is a director of two societies that are contracting with each other; or

(c) where a director learns of an opportunity for profit which might be valuable either to him personally or to another society (corporation) of which he is a member (this is known as a "corporate opportunity").

A director cannot put his personal interests ahead of the best interests of the society. If the society suffers damages as a result, he is liable to the society.

A director should not vote at a board meeting on any motion that might put him into a conflict of interest.

But this does not preclude him from voting as a member at a members' meeting in his own interest.

CHAPTER 7

Officers

¶ 700   Introduction

It is the officers who ultimately make the society come to life. No matter how idealistically the aims, purposes, and objects are expressed in the constitution, the society comes to life only when the officers start performing their duties, and it continues to exist only while the officers continue to perform those duties.

The functions and duties of the officers are the outgrowth of centuries of experience and experiments. While the functions and duties of each officer have become somewhat standardized, each society develops its own variations that are best suited to its purposes and its membership.

The basic officers are the president, secretary, and treasurer.

The officers may be known by other designations, or their functions may be re-distributed or combined by the constitution.

Other officers may be present in a society (for example, vice-president, assistant secretary, assistant treasurer, moderator, parliamentarian, etc.). One person may hold more than one office, and one office may be divided among one or more assistants. A moderator (*Rule 7.6*) may be appointed to chair one or more meetings in place of the president. A parliamentarian (*Rule 7.7*) may be appointed.

Rule 7.1   Election of Officers

In the direct model of organization (*see ¶ 105(i), Organization Models, page 4*), the officers are elected or appointed and are removable by the members (*see Rule 7.8*).

In the indirect model of organization, the officers are elected or appointed and are removable by the board.

The right to elect or appoint carries with it the right to remove. Whether an officer is appointed or elected makes no difference in the procedure for his removal. Unless he is removed from office, or unless his term of office is, in his appointment, expressly limited to a date, period of time, or event, an officer continues in his office until his successor is appointed or (if he was appointed by a board of directors) until the board which appointed him ceases to hold office. There should at all times be a president and a secretary. Under some constitutions, both offices may be held by the same person.

It is advisable to elect/appoint officers each year as soon as possible after the election/appointment of the board.

Rule 7.2   President

The president has more authority in the direct model of society organization (*see ¶ 105(i), Organization Models, page 4*) than in the indirect model (*ii*). In both cases, the president (who may be known under various titles, e.g., moderator or presiding officer) is the figurehead and the focus of all outsiders. Most constitutions provide that he is automatically a member of all committees. Unless the constitution provides otherwise, the president chairs all meetings of members and of the board (*see also Rule 7.6, Moderator, and Rule 7.7, Parliamentarian*).

In the direct model of organization (*see ¶ 105(i), Organization Models, page 4*), where the officers are elected directly by the members, the president may exercise more initiative. His primary responsibility is to the members. However, he is expected to follow the instructions of the board of directors, unless such instructions conflict with the wishes of the members.

In the indirect model of organization (*see ¶ 105(ii), Organization Models, page 4*), where the officers are elected or appointed by the board of directors, the president is responsible to the board and must comply with its directions.

Rule 7.3   Vice-President

In the absence of the president, the vice-president (if the society has one) assumes all the duties and responsibilities of the president.

When the president is chairing a meeting, and he wishes to participate in the discussion or propose a motion, the vice-president or a member (preferably an officer) will be called upon to substitute as Chair (*Rule 10.4, Temporary Chair, page 46*).

A society may have any number of vice-presidents — one for each of its functions.

Rule 7.4   Secretary

The secretary of the society performs many functions. Any one or more of these functions may be assigned to one or more assistants or employees. The various functions may be divided as follows:

1. As executive secretary, the secretary

- arranges the date and place of meetings of members;
- prepares the notice of meeting and the proxyform (if proxies are allowed);
- arranges for the printing and mailing of notices of meetings and proxyforms;
- arranges for receipt of proxies;
- assists in the preparation of the agenda;
- checks with officers and others to attend and bring reports (if any);
- attends meetings and assists the Chair;
- prepares formal minutes of the meeting;
- keeps available, at all relevant times, minutes of all meetings, lists of members, copies of the constitution (*see Glossary, page xvii*), lists of committees, and personnel of committees;
- coordinates all functions of the committees.

2. As secretary of the board, the secretary

- arranges the date and place of meetings of the board;
- prepares the notice and the agenda (if either is required);
- attends meetings of the board if requested, takes notes of the meeting, and assists the Chair;

27

- prepares minutes of the meeting;
- maintains the board minute book.

3. As corresponding secretary (sometimes called the "scribe") the secretary

- conducts the official correspondence of the society;
- maintains records of all correspondence and important conversations.

4. As recording secretary (sometimes called the "clerk"), the secretary

- records all motions, passed and defeated;
- may record (with or without the use of an electronic recorder) all discussions that take place at general meetings;
- may list various ideas suggested by the members on the subject of the motions discussed, whether or not the ideas are formalized into motions.

Rule 7.5 Treasurer

The treasurer handles all money of the society. He has the responsibility to

- collect all dues and other income
- do all banking
- pay accounts
- supervise or do all bookkeeping
- prepare statements for submission to the board, the auditor, and the members
- prepare budgets

If the work becomes onerous, the treasurer may seek the assistance of one or more employees and a finance committee; however, the responsibility remains at all times with the treasurer.

It is recommended that all cheques, withdrawals, and other contracts for money be signed by two or three members of the finance committee. There may be several levels of signing authority: small amounts may need the signature of one employee; medium amounts, one employee and one or two members; larger amounts, three members, including the treasurer.

Rule 7.6 Moderator

If the constitution so provides, a society may appoint a non-member to act as moderator to chair a general or board meeting in place of the elected Chair.

The moderator must be neutral, unbiased, and fair, and must not enter into the discussion except to control the procedure of the meeting. Unless he is a member who is able to vote, he cannot vote, even to break a tie. He may be elected or appointed by a simple majority vote of the society for a single meeting or for a longer term.

Rule 7.7 Parliamentarian

A society may appoint a member or non-member to act as parliamentarian (also known as a "preceptor") for general or board meetings to advise the Chair and the meeting on the proper procedures to be followed in the conduct of the meeting. The parliamentarian must be generally familiar with parliamentary procedures and with the rules of order adopted by the society. He is elected or appointed by a simple majority vote for a single meeting or for a longer term.

Rule 7.8 Removal of Officers

Subject to provisions in the constitution that state the contrary, an officer (which includes a Chair) may be removed:

- by the members, if he was elected or appointed by the members or by the board;

- by the board, if he was elected or appointed by the board (as in the indirect model of organization — *see ¶ 105(ii), Organization Models, page 4).*

Even if the appointment was for "the ensuing year or until his successor is elected or appointed", he may be removed at any time, with or without cause. The prescribed procedures must be strictly adhered to.

Before proceeding with a motion to remove, it is prudent to advise the officer of the intention to remove him, and to give him the opportunity to resign.

(i) *Motion*

"That A.B. be removed from office, effective immediately." (The reasons for his removal may be added.)

(ii) *Characteristics*

A motion to remove an officer is a main motion (*see chart, inside front cover*) that

- requires seconding;
- is amendable as to effective date and recitals; and
- requires a simple majority.

The officer must be given reasonable notice of the motion and of the meeting at which the motion is to be considered.

(iii) *Notice of Removal*

The notice must include

- the date, time, and place of the meeting;
- the proposed motion for removal, or a summary of the motion;
- the nature of the alleged misconduct, if misconduct is being alleged;
- a statement advising the officer that he may attend the meeting, and make submissions in his defence; and
- a statement informing the officer that, if he does not attend, the meeting may proceed in his absence and he will not be entitled to any further notice.

(iv) *Rights at Meeting*

The officer is entitled to attend the meeting, speak on his own behalf, be represented by counsel or an agent, bring in documentary evidence (witnesses' statements, etc.), and hear all complaints against him. He is also entitled to make the final statement after everyone has spoken and immediately before the vote is taken.

(v) *Requisitioned Meeting to Remove Officers*

Some statutes governing incorporated societies authorize a small percentage of the members to requisition the calling of a general meeting to pass any motion that is connected with the affairs of the society and that is not inconsistent with the governing statute. This would include a motion to remove officers in the direct model of organization. (*See also ¶ 2920, Requisitioned Meetings, Motions, and Circulated Statements, page 158.*)

CHAPTER 8

Committees

¶ 800 Introduction

A committee is a body of one or more members to which the appointing body delegates one or more of its functions.

The committee system is a device whereby the work-load of the main body (the general membership, the board, or the executive committee) is lightened, and members are given the opportunity to become more involved in the affairs of the society and to contribute any specific expertise they may have. A smaller group permits greater freedom of discussion with less formality and more confidentiality. More time may be devoted to each subject. Committees serve as advisers, investigators, and assistants to the president and the board.

A committee reports to the appointing body to which it is responsible.

Rule 8.1 Types of Committees

(a) Standing committees are permanent unless the constitution provides otherwise. They include

- the board
- the executive committee
- the membership committee
- the finance committee

31

and may include

- a nominating committee
- a program committee
- a special task committee

(b) Special committees are appointed for a special task and remain in existence only until their task is concluded and they report to the body which appointed them.

Rule 8.2 Standing Committees (Permanent)

The following aspects of standing committees are usually set out in the constitution:

- function or purpose (terms of reference);
- methods of selection of members (by election, appointment, or *ex officio*);
- right to make and implement decisions, or to make recommendations only;
- number of members, and procedure to fill vacancies;
- quorum for meetings (if not a majority).

Any aspect of a committee not included in the constitution may be added in the resolution activating the committee. The following aspects are usually added in the resolution activating the committee:

- name of Chair, or procedure to appoint Chair
- date of first meeting
- date of report submissions
- budget and expenses, if any, or limitations on spending

The following aspects may also be added in the resolution activating the committee:

- meetings via telephone
- question of coordination with any other committee.

(i) *Resolutions*

"Resolved, That

1. a [*type*] committee be approved, to be comprised of [*number*] members to [*purpose*] and to report back on [*date* or *event, or* at the next meeting, *etc.*];
2. the committee meet not later than [*date*] and report back before [*date*];

3. the committee be given a budget of $.... to be disbursed under the supervision of the treasurer."

The personnel of the committee may be elected or appointed — *see Rule 8.4(i).*

(ii) *Procedure*

A resolution to activate a standing committee

- is debatable
- is amendable, pertaining to items in Rule 8.2(i) only (and except items 1, 2, and 3), and
- requires a simple majority

Rule 8.3 Special Committees (*Ad hoc*)

A special committee ought not to be appointed if the subject can be dealt with by a standing committee.

The function, term of office, and method of selection of members is set out in the resolution creating the committee. The term of office expires when the committee's function is completed or, if the committee was created by the board, when the new board is elected or when the committee's function is completed (whichever occurs first).

The resolution creating a special committee may have all the aspects listed in Rule 8.2.

A special committee must submit a report, interim or final, to the body which created it, before the date of every annual meeting and when required by the appointing body.

Rule 8.4 Members of Committees

Members of a committee may be named or designated in the resolution creating or activating the committee (*Rule 8.2*), or in the constitution. If the committee is not fully named, or vacancies occur, any vacancies may be filled by the remaining members of the committee or by the body appointing it (unless the constitution provides otherwise). Often the Chair asks for volunteers and then asks for a motion to appoint them to the committee. The body appointing the members of the committee may appoint a Chair of the committee, or may leave it to the committee to appoint its own Chair. If no Chair of the committee is designated by the appointing body, the first-named member of the committee acts as temporary Chair until the committee elects a permanent Chair. The committee may also appoint its own secretary.

(i) *Motions*

"Resolved, That

1. A, B, C, D, and E be named to the [*name*] committee; *or*

2. A act as Chair of the [*name*] committee with authority to name the [*number*] other members; *or*

3. I, [*mover*], act as Chair of the [*name*] committee with two members of the [*another committee*] and two members whom I will select [*or*, and F and G]."

(ii) *Procedure*

A motion to appoint personnel to a committee in any of the ways specified above

- is debatable as to the examination of the recommendations, but not to the recommendations themselves;

- is not amendable; and

- requires a simple majority.

Personnel may also be elected to the committee (*see Chapter 24, Elections and Appointments, page 127*).

(iii) *Ex Officio Officers*

If the constitution provides that certain officers of the society are automatically members of all or certain committees, those officers remain members of the committee only while they retain such offices. Their successors will automatically become members of the committee.

Some constitutions provide that the treasurer is automatically a member of the finance committee, or that the president is automatically a member of all standing and special committees.

If the constitution designates certain officers of an outside organization (an associated society or a government body) as members of certain committees, those officers may retain membership in the committee only while they retain the office which qualified them to be on the committee (*ex officio*).

Rule 8.5 Powers of Committees

No committee has inherent rights and duties. It has only those rights and duties properly and specifically delegated to it by the constitution or the body appointing it.

Rule 8.6 Sub-Committees

Sub-committees may be appointed by a committee to deal with matters that may be dealt with more conveniently by one or two persons, such as interviewing a person, drawing a report, or investigating a matter. A sub-committee reports back only to the committee that appointed it. All the rules which apply to standing and special committees apply to sub-committees.

Rule 8.7 Reports of Committees

Committee reports should be addressed to the body which created the committee, and should contain the following information:

- when and how the committee was created;

- names of the members of the committee;

- terms of reference and background which led to the creation of the committee;

- a review of the work done by the committee (the evidence collected, the persons interviewed);

- conclusions and recommendations, including motions to be proposed.

The body to which the report is submitted may, with the appropriate resolution, receive, consider, adopt, reject, delay, postpone, or ignore the recommendations, or refer the report back to the committee (or to another committee) for further study.

(i) *Resolutions*

"Resolved, That

1. the report of .... committee be received (*or* accepted) for consideration; *and*

2. and that the recommendations contained therein be adopted and implemented; *or*

3. and that the recommendations relating to [*subject*] be adopted, but the recommendations relating to [*subject*] be rejected; *or*

4. and that the report be sent back to the committee for further consideration; *or*

5. and that the recommendations in the minority report be adopted and implemented."

(ii) *Procedure*

A motion to deal with a committee report in any of the ways specified above

- is debatable and amendable as to the adoption or non-adoption of the report, but not as to the recommendations themselves; and

- requires a simple majority.

(iii) *Minority Reports*

If one or more members of a committee disagree(s) with the majority, he/they may submit a minority report, signed by the dissenter(s). The minority report is submitted, at the same time and in the same manner as the majority report, to the body which created the committee. Either report, or parts of either report, may be adopted by the creating body (*see (ii), above*).

(iv) *Form*

"The undersigned, a minority of the [*name*] committee appointed to [*purpose*] not agreeing with the majority, desire to express our views on the subject as follows": [*continue with minority report*].

Rule 8.8 Termination of Committees

Upon the presentation of its report (or reports), the committee is automatically dissolved unless it is a standing committee. A special committee may be dissolved at any time by the body which created it.

CHAPTER 9

Committee of the Whole

¶900 Introduction

A committee of the whole is not strictly a committee, but it acts with all the informality of a committee. The name derives from Parliament resolving into a "Committee of the Whole House". It is a device to bring the entire membership body into the discussion and decision-making process by spending less time on formalities and more time on actual business.

Rule 9.1 Resolving into Committee of the Whole

When a meeting of members desires to discuss a complex, lengthy, or controversial question, it may, by resolution, resolve itself into a committee of the whole, thereby eliminating strict procedural rules and expediting the discussion and resolution of the question.

(i) *Motion*

"Resolved, That this meeting recess and resolve itself into a committee of the whole to consider -----." (Words may be added to limit the time for deliberation as well as the number and duration of speeches by any member, and to specify when to report back.)

A motion to delay or postpone discussion on the subject takes priority over a motion to resolve into a committee of the whole, even if the motion to resolve has already been passed.

(ii) *Characteristics*

A motion to resolve into a committee of the whole

- is not in order if there is a pending motion to adjourn the meeting or postpone discussion on the subject;
- requires seconding;
- is not debatable; and
- is amendable only as to the scope of the subject to be discussed and the name of the proposed Chair.

See (iii), below, for procedure in committee of the whole.

(iii) *Procedure*

1. On the passing of a motion to resolve the meeting into a committee of the whole, the Chair declares

   "This meeting is recessed until the committee of the whole submits its report."

2. The Chair appoints another member as temporary Chair and retires among the members. He may participate as a member.

3. The temporary Chair calls the meeting to order and asks the meeting if it wishes to elect a new Chair. If so, an election is held (*see Chapter 24, Elections and Appointments, page 127*). If there is no opposition, he remains as Chair of the committee of the whole.

4. The Chair restates the main motion (if there was one) or asks for a main motion on the subject.

5. Discussion is then open and is conducted informally. Motions need not be seconded. The Chair of the committee (as well as the Chair of the main meeting) may actively participate in the discussion and may move motions. Unless the resolution creating the committee of the whole imposes restrictions, there are no restrictions, within reason, on the number of times a member may speak, nor on the duration of his speeches, except that priority is given to a person who has not yet spoken.

6. When the deliberation is concluded, the committee moves:

   "Resolved, That this committee rise and report."

   This motion does not require seconding, and is neither debatable nor amendable.

7. Upon the passing of this resolution, a report is drawn up and submitted to the Chair of the main meeting, who then reconvenes the main meeting. (*See Rule 8.7, Reports of Committees, page 35.*)

8. A committee of the whole cannot adjourn or terminate; it can only report back to the main assembly. It may, however, recess for a few minutes to write its report.

A simpler method of accomplishing almost the same result would be to pass a resolution at a general meeting of the members as follows:

> *"Resolved, That the rules of procedure be suspended for the purpose of considering a motion to* [purpose] *and that the suspension be lifted at* [time]." (See Rule 9.2.)

Rule 9.2 Suspending the Rules

A motion to suspend the rules of procedure may be made:

- to permit some item to be taken up out of its scheduled order;
- to modify some procedure which interferes with the meeting's wishes, but which is not in conflict with the constitution;
- to discuss a subject that is very controversial or complex that would be hampered or delayed by strict adherence to rules of order.

(i) *Characteristics*

A motion to suspend rules:

- applies only to rules of procedure, not to bylaws;
- may be made at any time when no motion is pending, or while a motion is pending, if the motion to suspend is connected with and is restricted to the pending motion;
- yields to any other procedural motion, any closing motion, or any demand (*see chart, inside front cover*);
- does not allow speaker to be interrupted;
- requires seconding;
- is amendable only as to the scope of the subject to be discussed and the name of the proposed Chair;
- is not debatable;
- is not applicable with any motion except a motion to withdraw;

- requires a simple majority unless the subject-matter of the main motion requires a two-thirds or greater majority, in which case the motion to suspend requires the same majority.

(ii) *Form*

"I move that the rules of procedure be suspended until [*time*] for the purpose of discussing a motion to [*purpose*], and that the meeting resume not later than [*time*] today."

(iii) *Chair*

"It has been moved and seconded that the rules of procedure be suspended until [*time*] for the purpose of discussing a motion to [*purpose*] and that this meeting resume not later than [*time*]. All in favour? ------ All against? ------ The motion is carried. The rules of procedure are suspended in accordance with the resolution." (Traditionally, the Chair then retires and names a member to chair the meeting; *see Rule 9.1(iii) for procedure.*)

Rule 9.3 Reporting to the Meeting

Upon the passing of the motion to report, the committee of the whole is dissolved, and the Chair of the committee delivers the report to the Chair of the meeting with a motion to adopt.

"I move that the meeting adopt the report of the committee of the whole and of the following resolutions": [*list the motions passed by the committee of the whole*].

This motion does not require seconding, and is not debatable or amendable. It cannot be divided, but must be accepted or rejected completely. There is nothing to prevent a member from moving one of the resolutions included in the report if the report has been rejected.

PART II

ORGANIZATION OF MEETINGS

CHAPTER 10

The Chair

¶ 1000   Introduction

The word "Chair" covers both genders, as do "him" and "her".

Every meeting must have a presiding officer to ensure that proceedings are conducted in a proper and orderly manner. The presiding officer, however selected, is called the "Chair" and he always refers to himself as the "Chair", never "I". His main function is to keep the meeting going and to obtain the "sense of the meeting" in a legal and democratic manner.

The words "elected" and "appointed" are synonymous in connection with elections or appointments.

Any objection to the election of a Chair must be made at once; otherwise the election is deemed to be valid. An irregularity in his nomination or election that is not illegal may be cured by acquiescence.

A presiding officer cannot arbitrarily defeat the will of the majority by refusing to entertain or to put motions, by wrongfully declaring the result of a vote, or by refusing to permit the majority to express its will. The will of the meeting as legally expressed by a vote of the required majority is binding on the presiding officer, and he must accept its decision.

Under some constitutions, a "moderator" may be appointed for one meeting or for one year or longer. As a non-member he is neutral and therefore may not enter into the discussion or cast a vote, not even to break a tie. He is merely a traffic cop who keeps the traffic moving and avoids collisions.

Rule 10.1 Chair at Meetings

(i) *Members' Meetings*

The person named by the constitution as presiding officer for meetings of members shall preside as Chair; failing him, the president or vice-president (in order of priority) shall fill the position.

(ii) *Board Meetings*

The Chair is appointed by the members, in the case of a society based upon the direct model of organization (*see ¶ 105(i), Organization Models, page 4*) or by the board, in the case of a society based upon the indirect model of organization (*see ¶ 105(ii)*).

(iii) *Committee Meetings*

The member named in the constitution or in the resolution creating the committee, or as appointed by the committee members, shall preside as Chair.

(iv) *Ex officio Chair*

If the constitution provides that the past president or some other designated person shall act as Chair, such person may act as Chair, whether or not he is a member of the society.

Rule 10.2 Duties of Chair

The prime duty of the Chair is to comply with the constitution and enforce the rules of order adopted by the constitution. (*See also Chapter 34, Advice to an Inexperienced Chair, page 201.*) Specifically, the Chair must

1. Before the Meeting

- be fully cognizant of the society's constitution and the rules of order it has adopted;

- understand the spirit as well as the letter of parliamentary law and the rules of order;

- ensure that everyone entitled to be present has been notified;

- prepare or obtain an agenda and notice of the meeting, and proof of service of the notice on all persons entitled to notice.

2. At the Meeting

- call the meeting to order;

- ensure that reasonable accommodation is provided for all who are entitled to be present, and that everyone can see and hear the proceedings and participate therein;

- ensure that all persons entitled to attend are admitted;

- ensure that the meeting is properly constituted and that someone (namely, the recording secretary) is taking notes of the proceedings;

- insist on, and conduct himself with discipline and dignity, preserve order and decorum, and adjourn the meeting if this becomes impossible (the Chair may interrupt a speaker in order to maintain order and decorum);

- act fairly, in good faith, and without malice;

- appoint scrutineers, if requested, and instruct them in their duties;

- decide who shall speak (introduce speakers, if they are indicated);

- keep the meeting moving (i.e., not allow any awkward intervals);

- receive motions and amendments, and ensure that they are clearly and properly worded;

- rule out of order any motion worded disrespectfully, or restate substantially a resolution previously passed (or defeated) or part of the constitution, otherwise out of order;

- rule out of order any amendment worded disrespectfully or irrelevant to the motion or otherwise out of order, restate an amendment or motion previously dealt with, or negate the motion;

- decide when to cease discussion and go to a vote, and what method of voting would be appropriate (*see Chapter 22, Voting Methods, page 115*);

- ascertain the sense of the meeting;

- declare the result of the vote;

- rule on all points of order;

45

- declare the meeting concluded after all business has been transacted.

3. After the Meeting

- ensure that proper minutes of the proceedings are prepared.

If the Chair fails to duly perform his duties, he may be removed by the members, the board, or by the committee that he chairs, as the case may be (*see Rule 10.5*).

The Chair's rulings approximate those of a person occupying a judicial or quasi-judicial position. His rulings may be appealed to the general meeting (*see Rule 10.9*) unless the ruling deals with a legal matter, e.g., validity of proxies, etc., in which case see Chapter 14, Proxies, page 69.

Rule 10.3 Substitute Chair of the Meeting

A substitute Chair shall be appointed when

- the duly appointed Chair (as designated in Rule 10.1) is absent, refuses to act or continue to act, or is removed;

- the Chair wishes to make a motion;

- he is the subject of a motion on the floor questioning or praising his actions or decisions; or

- he wishes to leave the meeting for a short while (instead of recessing).

To appoint a substitute Chair, a temporary Chair is first appointed and he chairs the meeting according to the procedure set out in Rule 10.4 until a substitute Chair is appointed.

The substitute Chair retires from the chair on the appearance and request of the person having a greater right to chair the meeting (e.g., the president or the vice-president). (*See Rule 10.7.*)

Rule 10.4 Temporary Chair of the Meeting

When a substitute Chair (Rule 10.3) is required, a temporary Chair takes over the meeting. He may be one named by the regular Chair or one selected by the meeting. Preference should be given to a member who holds some office in the society. He proceeds as follows:

1. The temporary Chair conducts the meeting until a substitute Chair is appointed.

2. He asks for nominations. Nominations need not be seconded unless required by the constitution. A member may not propose himself, but may vote for himself.

3. If only one person is nominated, the temporary Chair asks for a motion that the person nominated be declared the duly appointed Chair of the meeting (*see Rule 24.7, Appointments, page 133*).

4. If more than one person is nominated, a vote is taken and the member who receives the highest number of votes is declared the duly elected Chair of the meeting. (This does not affect the right of the permanent Chair to act as Chair at future meetings.)

5. The temporary Chair retires from the chair on the appointment of the substitute Chair.

Rule 10.5 Removal of Chair of the Meeting

The right to elect a Chair carries with it the right to remove him. If the meeting has lost confidence in the Chair, or if the Chair disqualifies himself through his actions by improperly adjourning the meeting, vacating the chair, refusing to comply with the constitution or the adopted rules of order, or refusing to entertain a motion that he vacate the chair, or if he otherwise frustrates the business of the meeting, the members may remove him and elect a new Chair from among the members present in accordance with Rules 10.3 and 10.4. (*For removal of the Chair of the society, see Rule 7.8, page 29.*)

(i) *Form*

"That the Chair does not possess the confidence of the meeting."

(ii) *Procedure*

1. The speaker and the discussion may be interrupted in order to move the motion to remove.

2. The motion to remove requires seconding.

3. As soon as the motion to remove is seconded, the Chair must appoint the officer next in priority (*Rule 10.3*), or have an election for a substitute Chair as his temporary successor for the purpose of processing the motion to remove. The Chair must then retire. He may defend his actions but not from the head table.

4. The motion to remove requires a simple majority.

5. The motion to appoint a temporary Chair requires a simple majority, unless the constitution requires otherwise.

If the motion to remove the Chair is carried, the temporary Chair proceeds to the appointment of a substitute Chair (*Rule 10.3*).

If the Chair refuses to appoint a temporary Chair, the members may appoint one. If the original Chair refuses to leave the head table, the members may turn their chairs to face the temporary Chair, proceed to appoint a substitute Chair, and continue with the meeting.

A Chair who is removed cannot resume the chair for the remainder of the meeting, even though his right to vote is not impaired.

Rule 10.6 Vacating the Chair

If the Chair improperly vacates the chair or improperly closes the meeting, the meeting may, in the same or adjacent room, convene the meeting, appoint a substitute Chair (*Rule 10.3*), and continue with the meeting.

Rule 10.7 Chair to Continue

Subject to his being disqualified or properly removed (*Rule 10.5*), the Chair of the meeting, however selected (*Rule 10.1*), shall continue presiding throughout the meeting, including adjournments thereof. But on the appearance and request of a person having a greater right to preside, the temporary or substitute Chair shall retire from the chair.

Rule 10.8 Chair's Rights at Meetings

(i) *Moving, Seconding, and Discussing Motions*

The Chair of a general meeting or board meeting cannot move or second a motion or amendment while occupying the chair. An exception occurs when only one other qualified person is present at the meeting, in which case he may do so. If there are only two qualified members present, the Chair may move or second the motion.

At large auditorium-type meetings, the Chair should not enter into any discussion of the merits of a motion. If he wants to discuss the merits of a motion, he must vacate the chair and appoint a temporary Chair (*see Rule 10.4*).

In small round-table meetings, the Chair may participate in discussion of the merits of a motion, if no one objects. If anyone does object, the Chair should "vacate" the chair and appoint a temporary Chair. However, at this type of meeting, the Chair need not physically leave his chair when "vacating" the chair; the temporary Chair may preside from his own seat at the table.

(ii) *Voting*

Unless the constitution provides otherwise,

    (a) the Chair of a *members' meeting* is entitled to vote on a motion, if he has a vote as a member (even if this creates a tie vote);

    (b) the Chair of a *board meeting* is entitled to vote on a motion, if he is a director (even if this creates a tie vote); and

    (c) the Chair of a *committee meeting* is entitled to vote on a motion, if he has a vote as a member.

The Chair should abstain from voting on a "quick vote" (show of hands, etc.), except in the event of a tie vote.

(iii) *Casting Vote*

Some constitutions provide that the Chair of a meeting, if entitled to vote, is also entitled to cast a second or "casting" vote in the event of an equality of valid votes. The Chair cannot, however, use his casting vote to create a tie, only to break a tie.

Section 49 of the *Canada Act* (formerly the *British North America Act*) provides that the Speaker of the House of Commons does not vote except in the case of a tie.

(iv) *Committee Meetings*

The Chair of a committee meeting may move motions, vote, and otherwise participate fully in the meeting. In the case of a tie vote, he does not have a casting vote.

Rule 10.9 Appeals from Rulings of the Chair

Rulings of the Chair relating to procedural matters may be appealed to the meeting and reversed or varied by a majority vote of members. (Examples: point of personal privilege, point of general privilege, point of information, point of procedure, point of order, object to consideration, count quorum, recount (or revote) on a vote, order of the day, correct error.)

Decisions relating to the legality of proxies, ballots, or the results of polls are matters of law and are not appealable to the meeting; an error in the counting (see Rule 23.9, Recounts and Revotes, page 125) *may be appealed to the meeting.*

(i) *Motions* (by a member)

"I wish to appeal against the ruling of the Chair for the following reasons": [*reasons, in brief*], *or*

"I move that the Chair's ruling be dissented from", *or*

"I challenge the Chair."

The Chair shall put this motion to the meeting in the positive form:

"Resolved that the ruling of the Chair be upheld."

(ii) *Characteristics and Procedure*

A motion to appeal rulings of the Chair

- must be made immediately;
- requires seconding;
- is not debatable (however, the challenger may state his reasons for disagreeing, the Chair may give his reasons for the decision, and the challenger may reply in brief);
- requires a simple majority.

If no member asks for a poll, the Chair may rely on a voice vote; those supporting the rule vote "yes", and those against the rule vote "no". A tie vote supports the Chair in favour of his ruling.

After the vote, the Chair will declare either

"The ruling of the Chair is sustained", *or*

"The ruling of the Chair is reversed."

The Chair must comply with the decision of the meeting. If he refuses to comply after a negative vote, he may be removed under Rule 10.5.

If a member believes that a decision of the Chair or of the meeting is oppressive or unfair, he may apply to the courts for an order to rectify the matter.

Demands (points of order, privilege, etc.) are sometimes erroneously called "Appeals". See Chapter 21, Interrupting Discussion — Demands, page 109.

CHAPTER 11

Meetings

¶ 1100   Introduction

Meetings may be decision-making or informational, or both. Decision-making meetings must be conducted in a formal atmosphere in order to comply with the law and the adopted rules of order. Informational meetings are merely gatherings to pass on information or to seek information for future planning. These "rap sessions" may be conducted in an informal manner, since no binding resolutions are passed. Meetings may therefore consist of formal and informal sessions; conventions also consist of both.

A general meeting is a meeting to which every member in good standing is invited. Depending on the purpose of the meeting, it may be an annual (general) meeting, an ordinary (general) meeting, a special (general) meeting, or a meeting of a section of the society or of a class of members.

Rule 11.1 Rights of Members at Meetings

In the absence of specific rules or regulations to the contrary, members have the following rights with respect to meetings:

- to receive notices of meetings a reasonable (prescribed) time in advance;

51

- to attend meetings and be provided with adequate room, comfort, and facilities to hear and participate in proceedings;

- to enter into discussions;

- to propose motions and amendments;

- to question the Chair and movers of motions;

- to raise points of order and privilege;

- to vote on motions (voting rights may, under some constitutions, be limited to certain classes of members);

- to nominate candidates and be nominated for office (some constitutions may limit the right to certain classes of membership);

- to appoint proxyholders (if allowed under the constitution), revoke proxies, and reappoint proxyholders.

Rule 11.2 Control of the Meeting

Some questions relating to the conduct of the meeting are under the control of those properly present at the meeting and entitled to vote. They can determine

- whether notices, resolutions, minutes, and financial statements are to be read;

- whether strangers, representatives of the press, or other persons not entitled to be present, are to be permitted to attend;

- whether scrutineers should be appointed;

- whether and when discussion is to be terminated;

- whether and when the meeting is to be adjourned, and for what period;

- whether and when the meeting is to be concluded;

- whether and to what extent the auditors of the society may be questioned.

If necessary, the Chair shall take a vote to ascertain the sense of the meeting. The opinion of a majority is sufficient. The Chair may make a ruling on any of these matters, but may be overruled by a majority vote of the meeting. In the alternative, the Chair may ask for a motion from the floor instead of making a ruling himself.

Rule 11.3 Irregularities

The meeting must be called and held in strict compliance with the governing statute and the constitution; otherwise the meeting and the business transacted may be invalid.

Acquiescence, whether expressed or implied, or delay in raising an objection, may operate as an estoppel or may be deemed to be ratification.

Some irregularities may be cured or waived by the acquiescence of the members affected, but such acquiescence will not enable a society to do an act which is illegal or beyond the scope of its authority.

Rule 11.4 Annual Meetings of Members

Every society must have an annual meeting of members once a year, at which certain prescribed business must be transacted. Unless otherwise provided in the constitution, the annual meeting deals with

- reports of the board

- reports of committees

- financial statements

- election of directors

- election of officers, directors, and committees, if the structure of the society is based upon the direct model (*see ¶ 105(i), Direct Model, page 4), and*

- appointment of auditors or accountants

Rule 11.5 Ordinary Meetings

Ordinary meetings of members are meetings convened to deal with routine business other than the business of an annual meeting.

Ordinary business may be dealt with at annual meetings if proper notice has been given (*see Chapter 12, Notice of General Meetings, page 59*).

When the bylaws require meetings to be held on a regular basis (monthly, quarterly, etc.), they may be held together with or consecutive to annual or special meetings.

Rule 11.6 Special Meetings

Special (or extraordinary) meetings are meetings at which special (not routine) business is dealt with.

Special business may be dealt with at annual meetings if proper notice has been given (*see Chapter 12, Notice of General Meetings, page 59*).

The same notice may convene an annual meeting to be followed by a special meeting if proper notice of the business to be dealt with has been duly given.

Rule 11.7 Requisitioned Meetings and Circulated Statements

(a) *Use of Requisition*

The use of requisitions to force (i) a meeting to be called, (ii) notice of a proposed motion to be circulated to the members, or (iii) a statement to be circulated to the members, is becoming more common.

(i) *Requisitioning a Meeting*

In many societies, the constitution (including the governing statute and the bylaws) gives members having the right to vote the right to cause a meeting to be convened, upon delivery of a "requisition" (petition) containing the signatures of a small percentage of them.

(ii) *Requisitioning a Motion*

A similar requisition may be used to cause the board to give to all members having the right to vote notice of any motion that may be properly moved and is intended to be moved by the board at the next meeting of members.

(iii) *Requisitioning Circulation of a Statement*

Some constitutions give the members the right to have distributed by the society a statement relating to the business to be transacted at the next meeting of members.

(b) *Conditions*

(i) *Compliance*

The constitution (including the governing statute and bylaws) that authorizes requisitioned meetings, circulated statements, and motions, must be complied with strictly.

(ii) *Contents of Requisition*

The requisition should set out the nature of the business proposed to be dealt with at the meeting and the wording of the proposed motions.

(iii) *Signatories to Requisition*

The requisition should be signed by all the requisitionists, who must each be members having the right to vote at the proposed meeting. Not all the signatures need be on one document — any number of copies may be used.

(iv) *Calling Requisitioned Meeting*

Upon deposit of the requisition (in accordance with the constitution), the board shall forthwith call the meeting for the transaction of the business stated in the requisition.

(v) *Failure to Call Meeting*

If, within the time prescribed by the constitution, the board fails to call and hold the meeting as requested, any of the requisitionists may call such a meeting.

(vi) *Conduct of Meetings*

Requisitioned meetings shall be conducted under the same rules of order and practice as special meetings of the society are conducted.

(vii) *Reimbursement of Expenses*

Some constitutions also provide for the payment or reimbursement of the expenses arising from the requisition.

Rule 11.8 Reconvened Meetings

A reconvened meeting is deemed to be a continuation of the original meeting.

No new business (requiring notice) that is not covered in the notice of the original meeting may be transacted unless a new and proper notice is given. (*See Rule 12.8, Notice of Adjourned Meeting, page 63.*)

By participating in a reconvened meeting, the members are deemed to have waived any irregularity in the adjournment.

A member who objects may attend the reconvened meeting, object to the adjournment, and request that his objection be recorded in the minutes. (See Rule 12.9, Waiver of Notice, page 64.)

Rule 11.9 Board Meetings

Unless the constitution provides otherwise, meetings of the board of directors are convened by the board, and may be convened on a regular basis on a given day of the week or month, or when required.

Most bylaws provide for meetings to be called by the president or another specified officer (usually the vice-president or secretary) or by any two (or three) directors.

In the absence of provisions to the contrary in the governing statute or constitution, notice of the time and place of meetings of the board of directors must be given to all directors, otherwise the business transacted thereat is invalid.

Only directors may attend board meetings, but the board may permit experts, consultants, or others to attend. A motion passed by a majority vote is sufficient.

Notice of the business to be transacted at meetings of the board is not necessary in the absence of special provisions to the contrary in the constitution. If permitted by the constitution, no notice is required for the first meeting of the board of directors held immediately following the annual meeting for the purpose of electing and appointing officers, if all the directors are present or have waived notice.

Proxies are not permitted at board meetings unless specifically provided for in the constitution.

Once a notice of the meeting of the board or a committee is served, it cannot be recalled or postponed by another notice unless all the persons entitled to attend waive notice in writing. The meeting must be convened and then adjourned in the regular manner.

Rule 11.10 Committee Meetings

Unless the constitution provides otherwise, committee meetings may be called by the Chair of the committee, any two members of the committee, the body which created the committee, or the Chair of the body which created the committee.

Committee meetings may be convened on a regular basis or when required.

CHAPTER 12

Notice of General Meetings

¶ 1200   Introduction

Members' meetings are often referred to as "general meetings" to distinguish them from meetings of specific groups within the membership (for example, meetings of the board or meetings of committees).

The notice of a members' meeting is an important document. It sets limits on the business that may be transacted at a meeting, and may even affect the validity of the meeting. If the notice does not comply with the statutory requirements and the constitution, then the proxies, the resolutions, or the whole meeting may be invalidated.

The following items of business must be specifically referred to in the notice of meeting; they cannot be discussed or added to the agenda at the meeting as "new" or "other" business, unless all members (present and absent) waive notice:

- amendments to the constitution or bylaws;

- money resolutions — budgets, fees, borrowings;

- motion to reconsider a resolution previously passed or a motion previously defeated;

- annual meeting business (election or appointment of directors, officers, auditors, accountants, approval of financial statements, etc.);

- motions dealing with membership (admission, expulsion, rights or responsibilities of members), unless delegated to the board or a committee;

- removal of a director or officer;

- authorization to sell substantial assets of the society or to wind up the society.

Some of these items may be dealt with at board meetings if the constitution so provides, in which case no detailed notice of meeting is necessary, except in the case of a motion to remove an officer (*see Rule 7.8, Removal of Officers, page 29*).

Rule 12.1 Calling the Meeting

The meeting must be called and held in accordance with the constitution. An inherent irregularity in connection with the calling of the meeting invalidates the business transacted (*see Rules 12.2 to 12.10, below*).

Rule 12.2 Contents of Notice

(i) *Essential Provisions*

In the absence of special provisions in the constitution, notices of meetings must

- contain the date, time, and place of meeting (*see Rule 12.5, below*);

- in the case of meetings of members, set out the nature of all the business to be transacted at the meeting, either in full or in sufficient detail for the members to be able to determine whether to attend the meeting or appoint proxies (where proxies are authorized), and what preparations to make;

- contain the signature of the person or persons having authority to call the meeting;

- contain the names and offices of the person(s) calling the meeting (*see Rule 12.3, below*).

(ii) *Invalid Provisions*

A notice may be effective even if it contains invalid provisions, provided that the invalid provisions are severable from the rest of the notice.

- Invalid items of business are usually severable. For example, if the constitution or statute provides that officers shall be appointed by the board of directors, then the appointment of officers should not appear as an agenda item in a notice of general meeting. Such provision is severable from the rest of the notice, provided that there are other valid agenda items in the notice.

- Invalid procedural matters (e.g., place or time of meeting not authorized by constitution) are usually not severable.

(iii) *Omitted Provisions*

The omission of an essential item in the notice of meeting will not invalidate the notice if none of the recipients of the notice could reasonably be misled by the omission.

For example, if meetings are always held at the same place or the same time of day (either by the constitution or by custom), the omission of the place or the time of the meeting will not invalidate the notice.

(iv) *Optional Provisions*

One notice may call two or more separate meetings. However, this is not advisable.

(v) *Conditional Notice*

A notice must not be conditional upon the happening of some event unless such event directly affects the business to be transacted at the meeting.

- If the condition is not directly connected to the business to be transacted, the notice is invalid.

- A notice is valid if it is given for a meeting that is to be held in the event that a bylaw is enacted or confirmed at a prior meeting.

(vi) *Wording*

Notices must be simple, clear, and understandable. They need not be in any particular form, provided that they contain all the essential provisions. A sample form is included (*see Appendix A, Form S–1, page 205*).

Rule 12.3 Issuing of Notice

The notice must state the name(s) and office(s) of the person(s) calling the meeting.

If the board is calling the meeting of members, it must act as a board. One director or officer or even a quorum of directors will not suffice, but the board may direct any officer to issue the notice on behalf of the board.

The constitution may authorize one or more directors or officers to call a meeting of members.

In the case of a requisitioned meeting (*see Rule 11.7, Requisitioned Meetings and Circulated Statements, page 54*), at least the required minimum number of requisitioners must personally sign the notice.

The person who signs the notice must assure himself that he is properly authorized to sign.

Forms:

"By order of the board", per S . . . Secretary.

"By order of the president", per S.

"By D . . . and F . . .", directors of [*name of society*].

"By L, M, N, O, and P", the requisitioners.

Rule 12.4 Length of Notice

The constitution specifies how many days' notice of meetings must be given. If a shorter notice or no notice has been given, the meeting and all business transacted thereat are invalid, unless notice is waived by all persons entitled to receive notice.

If all members entitled to be present are present and do not object, or have waived notice, the meeting is valid.

In the absence of specific provisions in the constitution, the length of notice for meetings must be reasonable.

Rule 12.5 Date, Time, and Place

In fixing the date, time, and place for the meeting, consideration should be given to the nature of the organization, the distance that the members must travel, and the availability of the members.

If one meeting is to be held immediately after another meeting convened for the same day and place, the estimated time of the second meeting should be given, or the words "immediately following the (*annual*) meeting" should be added.

In the absence of specific provisions in the constitution, meetings should be held at the head or registered office.

A notice of meeting may be included in a newsletter or other mailing properly addressed, provided that all the requirements of notice are complied with (*Rule 12.2*).

Rule 12.6 Service of Notice

Notice must be served on all persons entitled to notice (*Rule 12.7*), either personally, or as provided in the constitution.

The constitutions of some societies require the notice of meeting to be published in a local newspaper.

If the notice is mailed, it should be addressed to the members at the address shown on the register of members. If this is done, the notice is validly served even if it is never received.

It is sufficient if the person who delivers or mails the notice proves service thereof by making and filing an affidavit or statutory declaration to that effect (*Appendix A, Form S–7, page 207*).

Rule 12.7 Persons Entitled to Notice

All members, including *ex officio* members, are entitled to notice of every meeting of their class of membership. Notices must also be sent to all other persons entitled to notice under the constitution: auditors, international or national affiliates, etc.

Where the membership is divided into different classes of members, (*see Rule 5.3, Classes of Membership, page 15*), and the constitution provides for separate meetings, only the members of the class that is meeting are entitled to notice.

For waiver of notice, see Rule 12.9.

Rule 12.8 Notice of Adjourned Meeting

When a meeting is adjourned for a period longer than the minimum length of time required to be given for notices of meetings, a notice of the adjourned meeting is required unless the constitution provides otherwise.

When a meeting is adjourned, no new business (that requires notice) not covered in the original notice may be transacted unless a new and proper notice is given.

When a meeting is adjourned due to lack of a quorum, a new notice is required unless the constitution provides otherwise.

Once a notice of meeting of members of the board or a committee is served, it cannot be recalled or postponed by another notice unless all the persons entitled to attend waive notice in writing. The meeting must be convened and then adjourned in the regular manner.

Rule 12.9 Waiver of Notice

Any person entitled to receive a notice of meeting may at any time, before or after the meeting, waive notice of the meeting and any irregularities in connection with the convening of the meeting. (*See Rule 16.3, Challenging Validity of Meeting, page 78.*)

By attending and participating in the meeting without raising objection, members are deemed to have waived notice. This applies to general meetings of members, board meetings, and committee meetings.

Proxyholders may waive notice of meetings (*Rule 14.4, Proxyholder Waiving Notice, page 71*).

CHAPTER 13

Agendas

¶ 1300   Introduction

An agenda is the official list and sequence of business intended to be dealt with at a meeting.

Agendas are prepared by the secretary in consultation with the person who will chair the meeting (president, Chair of the board, etc.) or other officer. If there is a chance that the meeting may be contentious, the society's lawyer should be consulted.

Rule 13.1 Agenda Items

An agenda listing the items of business intended to be conducted at the meeting, and the order of their presentation, must be prepared before the meeting. It should include any routine formal motions intended to be proposed. However, these may be omitted if the agenda is sent out with or included in the notice of meeting.

A proper agenda, like a restaurant menu, ought to prepare the readers (before or at the meeting) for the business to be discussed.

Rule 13.2 Distribution of Agenda

The agenda may be sent out with or included in the notice of meeting. Otherwise, it should be distributed at the meeting.

Members have a right to know in advance what items of importance will be considered at the meeting so that they may determine whether to attend, whether to appoint a proxyholder, and whether to conduct any research into the subject.

Rule 13.3 Approving the Agenda

The agenda should be presented for approval at the beginning of the meeting, at which time new items may be added, items may be deleted, renumbered, postponed, or made special orders (*see Rule 13.6, Special Order of the Day*).

Form:

"That the agenda as presented to the meeting be approved."

"That the distributed agenda for this meeting be approved."

Rule 13.4 Renumbering the Agenda (Order of Business)

The order of items on the agenda may be renumbered or changed by the Chair at any time if no member objects (*Rule 22.4, Acquiescence (Consensus), page 117*); they may also be changed at any time by resolution of the meeting.

(i) *Motions*

"If no member objects, we will take up Item 8 now instead of Item 4. We will then proceed with Item 4."

"I move that Item 6 be now considered."

"I move that Item 6 be taken up immediately after the election of the board."

"I move that Item 8 be taken up at 3:30 p.m. instead of 6:00 p.m. (*or, instead of its regular order*)."

(ii) *Procedure*

A motion to renumber agenda

- does not allow the speaker to be interrupted;
- requires seconding;
- is amendable only as to numbers of the items to be changed;
- is debatable only as to the reasons for the amendment;
- requires a two-thirds majority if the agenda had been distributed to the members before the day of the meeting; otherwise a simple majority will suffice.

Another way of accomplishing the same result, if a simple majority is in favour of the change, is to wait until Item 6 is opened for discussion, and then move to delay consideration of Item 6 until after Item 8 has been considered (after explaining the purpose). This motion requires only a simple majority instead of the usually required two-thirds. The same procedure is followed when Item 7 is opened for discussion. Then Item 8 comes up for consideration. *See also Rule 9.2, Suspending the Rules, page 39.*

Rule 13.5 Adding to the Agenda

New items may be added to the agenda by amendments to the motion to approve the agenda, or by separate motions.

(i) *Motion*

"That the agenda be amended by addition thereto as Item 7 [*describe item*] . . . and that the agenda as amended be approved."

This motion requires only a simple majority.

If the item proposed to be added is, in the opinion of the Chair, of a minor or routine nature, and the constitution does not require prior notice for such a motion, then the proposed item may be added to the agenda if no one objects or if a motion to add the item to the agenda is passed by a simple majority.

If the item proposed to be added is, in the opinion of the Chair, neither minor nor routine, or if the constitution requires prior notice for such a motion, the Chair should *not* add the item to the agenda, unless all members (present and absent) waive notice, or unless the statute or constitution provides that any matter relevant to the society may be raised at the meeting (e.g., *Ontario Condominium Act*, s. 18). *For examples of items that are neither minor nor routine, see the Introduction section (¶ 1200) of Chapter 12, Notice of General Meetings, page 59.*

However, the Chair may ask for a motion to refer such an item to the board of directors or to a committee to consider the issues and report back to a subsequent meeting.

Items for which a specific length of notice is required by the constitution cannot be added at the meeting.

(ii) *Procedure*

A motion to add to the agenda

- does not allow the speaker to be interrupted;
- requires seconding;
- is not amendable;
- is debatable, but only in respect of the amendment.

Rule 13.6 Special Order of the Day

A motion may be made a "special order" by naming in the motion, or in the notice of meeting or agenda, a specific time for its consideration, or a date and time, in the case of meetings lasting several days. This motion requires a simple majority.

The same result may be achieved by a separate motion made at the meeting. However, if the main motion has been circulated to the members before the day of the meeting (whether in the notice of meeting or in the agenda), it requires a two-thirds majority to make the motion a "special order".

(i) *Motions*

"---- and that this motion be considered on (*or* "be made an order of the day for [*date and time*]", *or*

"That Item 6 on the agenda be made a special order of the day for the next meeting [*or date*] at [*time*]."

(ii) *Procedure*

A motion to make a motion a special order of the day

- does not allow the speaker or discussion to be interrupted;
- requires seconding;
- is amendable only as to date and time;
- requires a two-thirds majority if the motion was listed on an agenda which was distributed to the members before the day of the meeting;
- takes precedence over all motions except a motion to adjourn and a question of privilege.

When the designated time arrives, the Chair, without interrupting any speaker having the floor, suspends discussion by saying

"The time has come for consideration of the special order of the day, a motion to [*describe motion, in brief*]. We will discontinue the present discussion on the current item until we have dealt with the special order."

If a member objects to consideration of an item on the agenda, he may vote against approval of the agenda, or wait until the item is announced by the Chair, and move a motion objecting to consideration under Rule 20.1, Objecting to Consideration, page 101.

CHAPTER 14

Proxies

¶ 1400   Introduction

(i) *Definitions*

- **"Proxy"** is a signed power of attorney appointing someone to act on behalf of a member at a meeting.

- **"Proxyform"** is an unsigned proxy.

- **"Proxyholder"** is the person appointed by a member as agent or attorney.

- **"Appointor"** is the person or entity appointing the proxyholder.

(ii) *Voting by Proxy*

There is no common law right to vote by proxy. Unless the constitution (*see Glossary*) specifically provides for it, voting cannot be done by proxy.

Where proxies are permitted, a member who has the right to vote (appointor) may appoint another person (proxyholder) to attend the meeting and to vote for him on his behalf at a general meeting of the society, and may instruct him how to vote on his behalf.

The constitution may determine the form of proxy, its maximum period of validity, whether the proxyholder need be a member, and when and where the proxies must be deposited.

Rule 14.1 Formal Requirements

If the constitution permits voting by proxy, but does not provide a specific form of proxy, the proxy should contain

- name of society;

- date of meeting, or method of fixing date of meeting;

- name or identification of proxyholder;

- date of proxy;

- signature of appointor.

The proxy may contain

- instructions directing the proxyholder to

    (a) vote for or against any motions,

    (b) vote for the election or appointment of any person(s), or

    (c) not to vote;

- authority of the proxyholder to waive notice or any irregularities in the calling of the meeting;

- authority of the proxyholder to attend, act, and vote for the appointor in the same manner as would the appointor if personally present;

- revocation of a previously given proxy.

Proxies may be limited as to time and as to the kind of meeting at which they are to be used.

The best practice is to have them for a specific meeting and adjournments thereof.

Rule 14.2 Signatures on Proxy

The Chair is not required to investigate the signature on the proxy. Unless he has evidence to the contrary, he may accept the signature as valid.

Proxies sent by fax machine (to the correct address) are acceptable.

If the appointor is a corporation, it is not necessary for a resolution of the appointor to be annexed to the proxy.

Rule 14.3 Deposit of Proxies

If the constitution requires the deposit of proxies a certain number of days before the meeting, this information must be annexed to the proxyform or included in the notice of meeting.

Rule 14.4 Proxyholder Waiving Notice

Proxyholders, if authorized by the documents appointing them, may waive notice of meetings and any irregularities in connection with the convening of the meeting for which they were appointed.

Rule 14.5 Revocation of Proxies

Proxies may be revoked by the appointor at any time, either by specifically revoking them, signing a new proxy, or attending and voting at the meeting.

Rule 14.6 Acceptance by Chair

The Chair determines whether to accept or reject any proxy. He is not obligated to accept the advice of the scrutineers or anyone else. He must, however, act fairly and listen to arguments in favour or against the acceptance or rejection of any proxy. Before accepting a proxy for filing, the Chair must satisfy himself that it conforms with the law (including the constitution, the governing statute, and the bylaws).

Rule 14.7 Possession of Proxies

Proxies, on being deposited, become records of the society. The Chair, the scrutineers, and all members entitled to vote, may examine them at all reasonable times before, during, or after the meeting. Adequate precautions should be taken to prevent tampering with or the disappearance of proxies. (The same rules apply to possession of ballots. A motion to destroy ballots after a reasonable period is sometimes acceptable, especially if no controversy is anticipated (*Rule 22.10(iii), page 120*).)

CHAPTER 15

Quorum

¶ 1500   Introduction

A quorum is the smallest number or proportion of members whose presence is required at a meeting in order that business may be validly transacted.

If the quorum is not stated in the constitution, it is fixed by common law at a majority of the members entitled to attend and vote at the meeting. It is not advisable to fix the quorum at a low figure as it may encourage bureaucratic government of the society, whereas a high figure might be unworkable.

A quorum is required (either by the constitution or common law) for all general meetings and also for board and committee meetings.

Rule 15.1   Quorum Present

Immediately after calling the assembly to order, the Chair shall take a quorum count. For this purpose he may rely on the secretary or the scrutineers at the door.

If the required quorum is not present within fifteen minutes (or such other time as is set out in the constitution), the Chair shall declare a lack of quorum. No official business may be conducted except to terminate the assembly, or adjourn the meeting to another date.

A proxyholder who is also a member is counted as only one person in a quorum at a meeting of members, regardless of how many members he represents. A proxyholder who is not a member is counted as one person in the quorum, regardless of how many members he represents, unless the constitution provides otherwise.

73

Rule 15.2   Quorum Count (Attendance)

At any time, at the beginning of or during the meeting, a member may question the existence of a quorum, and call for a count or recount. (This is a demand or question, not a motion.)

"Mr. Chair, is there a quorum present?" *or*

"Mr. Chair, I suggest the absence of a quorum."

If the Chair is satisfied that a quorum is present, he may reject the question; otherwise he shall order a count or recount. In the absence of evidence to the contrary, or a quorum count, a quorum is presumed to be present at all times.

In computing a quorum for attendance at a general meeting, the Chair may be included if he is a member in good standing and entitled to vote at that meeting. An *ex officio* member may be included if he has the right to vote, unless the constitution provides otherwise. A member who has a conflict of interest on any motion or in connection with any business transacted at a general meeting is included in the quorum count.

In computing a quorum for attendance at a board or committee meeting, every member of the board or committee who is present is included in the quorum. However, if a member of the board is in a conflict of interest situation with respect to a motion, he must disclose his interest, and must not be counted in the quorum. He must not participate in the discussion except to reply to requests for information, and he must not vote.

If the meeting lacks a quorum, it may be converted into an informational meeting (*see the Introduction section (¶ 1100) of Chapter 11, Meetings, page 51*), but no motions may be passed.

Procedure:

A demand for a quorum count

- can be raised at any time;

- allows the discussion, but not the speaker, to be interrupted;

- does not require seconding (it is not a motion);

- does not require a vote;

- allows the Chair's decision to be appealed to the meeting (*Rule 10.9, Appeals from Rulings of the Chair, page 49*).

Rule 15.3   Quorum Disappearing

Unless the constitution provides otherwise, a meeting cannot continue once a quorum disappears, even though it was validly opened with the required quorum. If no quorum count is taken or demanded, it is presumed that a quorum was present and continued to be present throughout the meeting.

Business transacted at a meeting which lacks a quorum is void. The presence or lack of a quorum may be determined from other sources if the minutes are not clear, e.g., a vote count recorded in the minutes, a roll call, admission list, etc. *See Rule 12.8, Notice of Adjourned Meeting, page 63, for notice of meeting adjourned by reason of lack of a quorum.*

A member who attends a meeting and withdraws is bound by the lawful acts of those who remain and carry on the meeting, provided that the quorum requirements have been satisfied. The withdrawing member is in the same position as the member who did not attend at all.

CHAPTER 16

Meetings of Members

Rule 16.1   Procedure for Opening Meetings

The procedure for opening a meeting of members are as listed below:

1. The Chair calls the meeting to order on time (*Rule 16.2*). (*See also Appendix A, Forms S–11, S–13, and S–15, pages 210 to 220.*)

2. If the secretary or recording secretary of the society is not present or does not wish to act as recording secretary at the meeting, a recording secretary is appointed (*Rule 7.4, Secretary, page 27*).

3. The Chair files proof of mailing (or other authorized form of service) of notice.

4. The Chair reports on attendance and states whether a quorum is present (*Rules 15.1, Quorum Present, page 73, and 16.6, Checking the Quorum*).

5. The Chair declares the meeting duly constituted. (*See Rule 16.7.*)

6. The Chair asks for a motion to approve the agenda (*see Rule 13.3, Approving the Agenda, page 66*).

7. The Chair asks for a motion to verify the minutes of the previous meeting (if required). (*See Rule 16.8.*)

Rule 16.2   Calling the Meeting to Order

The meeting should be opened at the time specified in the notice. If more members are expected, it may be delayed for not more than fifteen minutes. If the Chair is not present, a substitute Chair may be appointed (*see Rule 10.3, Substitute Chair, page 46*).

Chair:

"The meeting will now come to order . . . In accordance with the constitution, I will act as Chair [*or*, the Chair states his authority]."

Rule 16.3   Challenging Validity of Meeting

Any challenge to the validity of the meeting should be made at the opening of the meeting. Otherwise, those present may be deemed to have waived their right to question the validity of the meeting at a later time.

Rule 16.4   Appointing a Secretary

The secretary of the society may act as recording secretary of the meeting (*Rule 7.4, Secretary, page 27*). The Chair may, before or at the meeting, appoint a recording secretary. If any member objects to the person appointed, the Chair should request a formal motion and put the motion to a vote. (The motion may be to appoint the person whom the Chair has selected, or to appoint some other named person who is in attendance at the meeting.) Unless the constitution requires it, the secretary of the meeting need not be a member or officer of the society.

Chair:

"Mr. A will act as secretary of the meeting", *or*

"Would someone make a motion to appoint a recording secretary of the meeting?" (*Proceed as in Rule 24.7, Appointments, page 133.*)

Rule 16.5   Checking the Notice

Before proceeding with the meeting, the Chair must be satisfied that the notice is in order (*Rule 12.2, Contents of Notice, page 60*) and issued by the proper authority (*Rule 12.3, Issuing of Notice, page 62*), and sent in proper time (*Rule 12.4, Length of Notice, page 62*) to every member entitled to notice (*Rule 12.6, Service of Notice, page 63*).

The reading of the notice and proof of service does not validate an invalid or deficient notice (*Rule 12.2, Contents of Notice, page 60*). A motion to "take as read" or to "waive the reading" is unnecessary unless the constitution requires the notice to be read.

The notice and proof of service should be annexed to the minutes of the meeting.

Rule 16.6   Checking the Quorum

The Chair must satisfy himself that a quorum is present. If an exact count of the attendance has not been completed, he may wait for the actual count from the secretary or the scrutineers, or he may carry on the meeting until the count has been completed.

Chair:

"I have checked the attendance (*or*, I am advised that) and I declare that a quorum is present."

Rule 16.7   Meeting Duly Constituted

When Rules 16.4 and 16.6 have been complied with, the Chair may declare the meeting duly constituted for the transaction of business. (This is optional.)

Chair:

"I declare that this meeting is duly constituted for the transaction of business."

Rule 16.8   Verification of Minutes

Unless required by the constitution, the minutes of the previous meeting need not be read or verified. Verification of the minutes of the previous meeting is desirable, even if not strictly required.

(i) *Motion*

"I move that the minutes of the meeting of members held on [*date*] be taken as read and verified."

If the minutes are read or have been previously distributed, the Chair may ask whether there are any errors or omissions in the minutes (*Rule 27.5, Verification of Minutes, page 145*). Anyone who was present at the meeting, the minutes of which are under discussion, may point out errors or omissions, and move that the minutes be verified with or without correcting deletions or additions.

(ii) *Chair*

"You have received the minutes of the last meeting. Are there any errors or omissions? Will someone move that the minutes be verified?"

Rule 16.9   Appointing Scrutineers

The Chair may at any time, before or during the meeting, on his own initiative, or at the request of a member, appoint one or more scrutineers (counters) to assist him in taking the attendance and counting the proxies and ballots. If any member objects to the proposed appointment of a scrutineer, or to the person to be appointed, the Chair should request a formal motion and put it to a vote. Scrutineers need not be entitled to vote at the meeting, and should preferably be independent parties. (*See Glossary, page xvii.*)

Rule 16.10   Duties of Scrutineers

The scrutineers (counters) shall, as expeditiously as possible

(a) after checking the members present against the membership list or register, report the attendance at the meeting;

(b) collect, examine, and tabulate proxies (*Rule 14.1, Formal Requirements, page 70*), noting any special instructions or limitations;

(c) report in detail to the Chair;

(d) collect, examine, and tabulate ballots;

(e) report in detail to the Chair, noting any defective ballots or nonconformance with proxy instructions;

(f) return all proxies and ballots to the Chair for his perusal and custody.

The scrutineers' duties are ministerial, not judicial. They shall not question a proxy which, on its face, appears to be genuine and valid. They make no determination, but report all questionable proxies and ballots to the Chair for his decision.

The Chair is not obligated to accept the report of the scrutineers.

Rule 16.11   Discharging Scrutineers

On completing and submitting their various reports (*Rule 16.10*) to the Chair, scrutineers are automatically discharged.

Scrutineers, including those appointed by the Chair, may be discharged or replaced by the meeting at any time; only those appointed by the Chair may be discharged or replaced by the Chair at any time.

CHAPTER 17

Motions

¶ 1700 Introduction

The will of the meeting is determined and expressed by voting on proposals submitted for its consideration in the form of motions.

A motion is a proposal to do something, to order something to be done, or to express an opinion about something. The subject of a motion is "the question". A motion that has been passed becomes a resolution. Everything the society proposes to do requires a resolution. The resolution may authorize an officer or committee to do something on its behalf. A resolution applies to a single act of the society, in contrast to a bylaw, which is a permanent, continuing rule applied to all future occasions.

There are six different categories of motions:

- main motions (substantive), which originate business (*Rule 17.2*);

- amendment motions, which amend motions and resolutions (*Chapter 18, Amendments to Motions, page 91*);

- procedural motions, which direct the conduct of motions (*Rule 17.3*);

- demands (which are not truly motions) (*Chapter 21, Interrupting Discussion — Demands, page 109*);

- closing motions, which close the meeting, permanently or temporarily (*Chapter 26, Closing the Meeting, page 139*);

- elections and appointments (*Chapter 24, Elections and Appointments, page 127*).

Some statutes and constitutions require certain resolutions to be passed by greater than a simple majority:

- an extraordinary resolution requires more than a two-thirds majority (usually 75 to 95 percent);

- a special resolution requires a two-thirds majority;

- an ordinary resolution (all others) requires only a simple majority (half the votes plus one).

There can only be one main motion, procedural motion, demand, or closing motion on the floor at one time. Some motions may be interrupted for the purpose of considering a motion having a higher order of precedence (*see chart, inside front cover*).

Rule 17.1   Contents of Motions

Form:

All motions and amendments (*Chapter 18, Amendments to Motions, page 91*) begin with the word "that" and must be

- relevant to the subject under discussion

- within the power and scope of the meeting and the constitution

- in the affirmative

- not argumentative

- not offensive

- free from unnecessary words

- free from objectionable words

A motion may have a preamble beginning with the word "whereas" to explain its history or authority.

If the motion does not comply with all of these conditions, it is to be ruled out of order. Even if it complies with all but one condition, it is to be ruled out of order. Once a motion is declared out of order, it cannot be discussed or voted on. The same rule applies to amendments.

If the motion contains more than one proposition, the Chair may divide it into two or more motions (*Rule 17.9*). However, if any voter objects to the division, the Chair shall ask for a motion to divide.

A motion is expressed in one of the following forms:

1. "I move that . . ."

2. "I make a motion that . . ."

3. "I present a draft resolution to . . . and move that it be adopted"

Rule 17.2   Main Motions

Main (substantive) motions originate business, and direct, authorize, adopt, ratify, approve, confirm, or reject actions. Main motions may also be used to express an opinion of the meeting. Procedural, amendment, and closing motions and demands all have precedence over main motions (*see chart, inside front cover*).

A speaker or the discussion may not be interrupted for the purpose of moving a main motion. The main motion requires seconding, is amendable and debatable, and requires a simple majority unless the statute or the constitution provides otherwise. Procedural and amendment motions (except sub-amendments) can be applied to main motions.

Rule 17.3   Procedural Motions

Procedural motions are used to deal with, modify, or dispose of main motions. They have precedence over main motions.

The discussion may be interrupted for procedural motions, but not while a speaker has the floor. The procedural motions require seconding.

The following are procedural motions:

1. Objecting to Consideration (*Rule 20.1, page 101*),

2. Voting Immediately (*Rule 20.6, page 105*),

3. Closing the Discussion (*Rule 19.6, page 100*),

4. Postponing Discussion (To a Fixed Time) (*Rule 20.3, page 103*),

5. Postponing Discussion Indefinitely (*Rule 20.4, page 103*),

6. Referring or Referring Back (*Rule 20.7, page 106*),

7. Resolving into Committee of the Whole (*Rule 9.1, page 37*),

8. Suspending the Rules (*Rule 9.2, page 39*).

Rule 17.4   Demands

Demands concern the rights and privileges of members, and in no way affect the course of the main motion. They take precedence over main, amendment, and procedural motions (*see chart, inside front cover*).

The order of demands is based upon the order in which the movers are recognized by the Chair, except for quorum count, which has the highest precedence of all demands.

The following are demands:

1. Quorum Count (Attendance) (*Rule 15.2, page 74*),

2. Point of Personal Privilege (*Rule 21.2, page 110*),

3. Point of General Privilege (*Rule 21.3, page 110*),

4. Point of Information (*Rule 21.4, page 111*),

5. Point of Procedure (Parliamentary Inquiry) (*Rule 21.5, page 111*),

6. Point of Order (*Rule 21.6, page 112*),

7. Correcting an Error (*Rule 21.7, page 112*).

Rule 17.5   Closing Motions

Closing motions are motions dealing with the termination or suspension of the meeting. They have the highest precedence over all motions and demands.

The following are closing motions:

1. Concluding Meeting (*Rule 26.2, page 140*),

2. Adjourning Meeting to a Fixed Date (*Rule 26.3, page 140*),

3. Adjourning Meeting Without Fixed Date (*Rule 26.4, page 141*),

4. Recessing Meeting (*Rule 26.6, page 141*).

Rule 17.6   Right to Propose a Motion

A motion may be proposed by any person entitled to vote (except the Chair of the meeting, unless there are only two or three qualified voters present).

If the Chair wishes to propose a motion or an amendment (*Rule 10.3, Substitute Chair, page 46*), he should appoint a substitute Chair and then propose his motion from the floor. In the alternative, he may remain in the chair and ask another person to propose the motion.

If there are only two or three qualified voters present, the Chair may propose a motion (or amendment) without appointing a substitute Chair.

Rule 17.7   Proposing a Motion

The procedure for proposing a motion is as follows:

1. A member having the right to vote indicates to the Chair his desire for the floor (*Rule 19.4, Speakers, page 99*) and, when recognized, he rises and proposes the motion.

2. If it is a motion which requires seconding (*Rule 17.8*), the Chair asks for a seconder. If no seconder is forthcoming, the motion is rejected, unless the Chair dispenses with seconding or seconds the motion himself (*see Rule 10.8, Chair's Rights at Meetings, page 48*).

3. The Chair considers its relevancy and its form (*Rule 10.2, Duties of Chair, page 44*) and, if satisfied that it is in order, he calls for discussion on the motion. If it is not worded respectfully or if it is substantially the same as a motion already voted on at the meeting, or (if an amendment) if it negates the main motion, or if it is inconsistent with the constitution, or otherwise out of order, the Chair may rule the motion out of order.

4. If there is any confusion about the wording of the motion, or any doubt as to its exact meaning and effect, the Chair may ask the proposer to repeat, explain, clarify, or amend it.

5. When discussion has ended (*Rule 19.6, Closing the Discussion, page 100*), the Chair restates the motion (in its final form after all amendments) and decides upon the method of voting (*Chapter 22, Voting Methods, page 115*).

6. The vote is taken in accordance with one of the voting methods listed in Chapter 22.

7. The Chair declares the result (*Rule 22.12, Chair's Decision, page 121*).

Of the following categories of motions: main, procedural, demand, or closing, there can only be one motion of each on the floor at one time, although discussion may be interrupted on any motion (except a closing motion) for the purpose of moving, seconding, and discussing any motion having a higher precedence. (*See chart, inside front cover.*)

It is possible to have more than one amendment motion on the floor at one time; for example, an amendment, a sub-amendment, and a motion to withdraw the sub-amendment could all be on the floor at the same time.

Rule 17.8   Seconding a Motion

By universal practice, all closing motions (*Rule 17.5*), procedural motions (*Rule 17.3*), main motions (*Rule 17.2*), and amendment motions (*Chapter 18, Amendments, page 91, and Chapter 25, Reviewing Resolutions and Motions, page 135*) require seconding, unless the constitution provides otherwise.

Although it has become a universal practice, there is no requirement at common law for a motion to be seconded. It is a device to ensure that the motion has more than one supporter. If the motion is not seconded, the Chair has the right to assume that there is no interest in the motion, and he may refuse to accept it or to permit discussion on it. However, he may, if he wishes, second the motion himself in order to have it discussed and voted on. A seconder is not obligated to vote in favour of the motion which he seconded.

Where there are only two or three qualified voters present, the Chair may second a motion himself (*Rule 10.8, Chair's Rights at Meetings, page 48*) and bring it into the discussion stage.

Rule 17.9   Dividing a Motion

Motions are divisible. A motion shall contain only one proposition. When two or more propositions are contained in one motion and each one is so separate and distinct as to be complete in itself if the others are rejected, the Chair may divide them into separate motions and deal with each one separately, or he may divide them into separate paragraphs and deal with each paragraph separately. Division may be made by the Chair on his own volition, or on a demand or a motion by a voter. The consent of the mover or seconder of the original motion is unnecessary. If any member objects to the division, the Chair may ask for a motion to divide.

Discussion on the main motion may be interrupted for the purpose of a motion to divide, but not while a speaker has the floor. A motion to divide requires seconding and is not amendable. It may be debated only with respect to the wisdom of making the division, and it takes precedence over the main motion. It can be applied to all main motions and amendments which are divisible *and can have no other motion applied to it except a motion to withdraw.*

Voters may propose different divisions, and each proposal is dealt with in the order in which each is proposed until one is acceptable to the meeting.

Motion:

"I move that the motion be divided into two separate motions, one to read as follows: "that etc.," and the other to read as follows: "that etc.," *or* "I suggest (or request) that etc."

Rule 17.10   Withdrawing a Motion

The mover of a motion (or amendment) may withdraw or modify it before it has been stated by the Chair or seconded.

After it has been stated by the Chair, it can only be withdrawn with the unanimous consent of the meeting, or by a vote in favour of such withdrawal.

The motion to withdraw requires seconding and is not amendable or debatable. It takes precedence over all motions except closing motions, and can apply to any motion. A speaker may not be interrupted for the purpose of withdrawing a motion.

At the request of one or more members, the Chair may ask the meeting if it has any objection to the withdrawal of the motion. If there are no objections (complete acquiescence), permission is granted and the motion is withdrawn. If, however, there is even one objection, a vote must be taken on the motion to withdraw. If the motion to withdraw passes, the mover may withdraw the original motion. If the motion is defeated, permission is refused and the original motion must proceed despite the wishes of the mover.

When a motion is withdrawn, all motions applied to it collapse.

Motion (before seconding):

"Mr. Chair, I wish to withdraw my motion", *or*

(after seconding)

"Mr. Chair, I ask leave to withdraw my motion", *or*

"I move that Mr. A be permitted to withdraw his motion", *or*

(after being stated)

"Is there any objection to Mr. A withdrawing his motion?"

CHAPTER 18

Amendments

Rule 18.1   Amendable Motions

Amendments are motions to provide alternatives to the motion on the floor.

Some closing motions are not amendable, while others are amendable only partially:

1. Concluding the Meeting

   ● not amendable (*Rule 26.2, page 140*)

2. Adjourning the Meeting to a Fixed Date

   ● amendable as to time and place (*Rule 26.3, page 140*)

3. Adjourning the Meeting Without Fixed Date

   ● not amendable (*Rule 26.4, page 141*)

4. Recessing the Meeting

   ● amendable as to time and place only (*Rule 26.6, page 141; see also chart, inside front cover*)

Demands are not amendable (*Rule 21.1, Demands, page 109*).

Some procedural motions are not amendable, while others are amendable only partially:

1. Objecting to Consideration

   ● not amendable (*Rule 20.1, page 101*)

91

2. Tabling a Motion

   • amendable only as to time for resumption (*Rule 20.2, page 102*)

3. Postponing Discussion (to a fixed time)

   • amendable only as to time for resumption (*Rule 20.3, page 103*)

4. Postponing Discussion Indefinitely

   • not amendable (*Rule 20.4, page 103*)

5. Limiting Discussion

   • amendable only as to length and number of speeches and time for closing discussion (*Rule 20.5, page 104*)

6. Voting Immediately

   • not amendable (*Rule 20.6, page 105*)

7. Referring or Referring Back

   • amendable only as to conditions of reference (*Rule 20.7, page 106*)

8. Resolving into Committee of the Whole

   • amendable only with respect to the scope of the subject to be discussed and the name of the proposed Chair (*Rule 9.1, page 37*)

9. Suspending the Rules

   • amendable only with respect to the scope of the subject to be discussed and the name of the proposed Chair (*Rule 9.2, page 39*)

Of all motions that amend motions and resolutions, only amendments and sub-amendments are amendable (*Rule 18.3; see also chart, inside front cover*). The following motions are not amendable:

1. Dividing a Motion (*Rule 17.9, page 88*)

2. Withdrawing a Motion (*Rule 17.10, page 89*)

3. Reconsidering a Defeated Motion (*Rule 25.1, page 135*)

4. Reconsidering a Resolution (*Rule 25.2, page 135*)

5. Rescinding a Resolution (*Rule 25.3, page 136*)

6. Making a Resolution Unanimous (*Rule 25.4, page 137*)

Main motions are amendable (*Rule 17.2, Main Motions, page 85*)

Rule 18.2   Conditions of Amendments

A motion may be amended any number of times by adding, deleting, or substituting words or figures, but only one amendment to a motion or one sub-amendment may be on the floor at any one time.

An amendment to a motion or amendment must be relevant to the motion, and may be either compatible with or hostile to the motion. It cannot be of such a nature that the original motion (or amendment) loses its identity. If the proposed amendment does not comply with this rule, it is out of order.

An amendment to a motion or amendment must not be simply a negation of it. It must accomplish more than what a vote against the motion (or amendment) would accomplish. If the proposed amendment does not comply with this rule, it is out of order.

Only one amendment to the motion is in order at a time, but a sub-amendment to the amendment may be moved.

The mover of the original motion may voluntarily accept the amendment and modify his motion accordingly, if there is no objection from the meeting. However, once it has been stated by the Chair, the motion belongs to the meeting, not to the mover.

Sometimes a motion may be amended in such a manner as to defeat the motion on the floor by making it (the original motion with the amendments attached thereto) wholly unacceptable to the meeting. The use of an amendment for this purpose ("crippling amendment") is legally permissible. While a motion to amend may not merely negate the original motion, an amendment may be made that cripples the intent of the original motion so as to make it completely worthless or wholly unacceptable to the meeting.

For example, a motion to retain an investigator to examine the society's operations would become useless if an amendment were passed to restrict his fee to ten dollars per day. However, such an amendment would be in order and would have to be put to a vote. (For procedure, see (ii), below.) Of course, there is nothing to prevent the moving of a sub-amendment to fix the fee at some more reasonable figure.

(i)   *Characteristics of Motion to Amend a Motion*

- takes precedence over a main motion and motion to postpone indefinitely
- does not allow a speaker to be interrupted
- allows the discussion to be interrupted
- requires seconding

- is debatable as to the amendment only
- is amendable (by sub-amendment)
- requires the same majority as the main motion to which it is attached

(ii) *Procedure*

The procedure for amending a motion is as follows:

1. A motion to amend the motion under discussion is made by a person having the right to vote after he has been given the floor (*Rule 18.5*), and it is seconded (*Rule 17.8, Seconding a Motion, page 88*).

2. The Chair considers the relevancy (*Rule 17.1, Contents of Motions, page 84*) and the form (*Rule 18.1*) of the motion to amend, and, if satisfied that it is in order, he accepts it and calls for discussion on the amendment (*Chapter 20, Interrupting Discussion — Procedural Motions, page 101*).

3. If there is any confusion about the wording of the amendment, or any doubt as to its exact meaning and effect, the Chair may ask the mover of the amendment to repeat, explain, or clarify it.

4. Discussion is opened (*Rule 19.4, Speakers, page 99*). Discussion must be confined to the amendment only — not to the original motion.

5. When discussion is ended (*Rule 19.6, Closing the Discussion, page 100*), the Chair restates the motion to amend and decides upon the method of voting (*Chapter 22, Voting Methods, page 115*).

6. The vote is taken.

7. The Chair declares the result (*Rule 22.12, Chair's Decision, page 121*).

8. If the motion to amend is defeated or tied, the amendment is dropped and the original motion is proceeded with in the form originally proposed, as if no amendment had been proposed. (Before the amendment is voted upon, a sub-amendment (*Rule 18.3*) may be proposed and the same procedure followed.)

9. If the amendment is carried, the original motion is reworded to incorporate the amendment, and is then proceeded with in its amended form as if it were the original motion.

   "I move that the motion be amended by adding the words . . . before the word . . .", *or*

   "I move that the motion be amended by deleting the words . . .", *or*

"I move that the motion be amended by substituting the words . . . for the words . . . so that if the amendment is carried the motion will read . . . etc."

Rule 18.3   Sub-Amendments

An amendment may be amended any number of times, but only one amendment to an amendment (sub-amendment) is in order at one time. It must be relevant to, but not a negation of, the amendment it proposes to amend. The sub-amendment is voted on before the amendment. If the sub-amendment is carried, the original amendment is reworded accordingly. If it is defeated or tied, the sub-amendment is dropped and the original amendment remains on the floor, once again open for discussion and amendment.

Rule 18.4   Moving of Sub-Amendments

The procedure for moving a sub-amendment is identical to that for moving an amendment (*Rule 18.2, Conditions of Amendments*).

Rule 18.5   Voting on Sub-Amendments

If there is a motion for sub-amendment, it is voted on before the amendment is voted on. If the sub-amendment is carried, the amendment is reworded to incorporate the sub-amendment, and is restated by the Chair. Unless another sub-amendment is moved, the amendment is then proceeded with, following the procedure for dealing with motions.

¶ 1855   Examples

(i) *Motion*

"I move that the society investigate the opening of a branch in Edmonton" (*see procedure under Rule 17.2, Main Motions, page 85*).

(ii) *Amendment No. 1*

"I move that the motion be amended by deleting the words 'a branch in Edmonton' and substituting the words, 'branches in Edmonton and Victoria'."

Until this amendment is voted upon, no other amendment to the motion may be made, but a sub-amendment to the amendment is permissible.

(iii) *Sub-Amendment No. 1*

"I move that the amendment to the motion be amended by deleting the words 'Edmonton and Victoria' and substituting the words 'in every capital in Canada'."

Assuming that on a vote, Sub-Amendment No. 1 is lost, and on a vote, Amendment No. 1 is carried, the motion now reads as follows:

"That the society investigate the opening of branches in Edmonton and Victoria."

At this stage the motion may be amended.

(iv) *Amendment No. 2*

"I move that the motion be amended by adding the words 'and that the president be sent to Edmonton and Victoria for that purpose'."

(This amendment could not have been considered while Sub-Amendment No. 1 or Amendment No. 1 were on the floor. Amendment No. 2 may now be proceeded with.)

Assuming that Amendment No. 2 is carried, the motion now reads as follows:

"That the society investigate the opening of branches in Edmonton and Victoria, and that the president be sent to Edmonton and Victoria for that purpose."

(v) *Amendment No. 3*

"I move that the motion be amended by adding the words 'and the treasurer' after the word 'president'."

(This amendment could not have been considered until Amendment No. 2 had been dealt with.)

Assuming that Amendment No. 3 is carried, the motion now reads:

"That the society investigate the opening of branches in Edmonton and Victoria, and that the president and the treasurer be sent to Edmonton and Victoria for that purpose."

If a vote on the motion is carried, it becomes a resolution:

"Resolved, That the society investigate the opening of branches in Edmonton and Victoria, and that the president and the treasurer be sent to Edmonton and Victoria for that purpose."

CHAPTER 19

Discussion

¶ 1900   Introduction

Freedom of expression is a prime attribute of democracy and should be encouraged in society gatherings. In order to give every member an equal opportunity to speak and to be heard, rules of order have evolved. The larger the assembly, the more rigid should the rules be and the more strictly should they be respected and observed.

The conversation at small meetings, as at dinner parties, may be informal and uninhibited. Some members may wander off topic or talk too much; time and efficiency are not important. However, as the size of the gatherings increases, the necessity for rules becomes more apparent. It is the duty of the Chair to stop some speakers, redirect others, and generally encourage the expression of different views on the subject. Some societies limit the length of time a member may address the Chair (the meeting). This limitation may be in the bylaws or in standing orders or rules.

In this text, "debate" and "discussion" are synonymous. By tradition, some motions (*see Chapter 17, Motions, page 83*) are fully debatable, some are debatable as to time and place only, and some as to date and time only. Other motions are not debatable at all (*see chart, inside front cover*).

While free discussion is to be encouraged, there are parliamentary devices by which discussion may be deferred, avoided, interrupted, or even terminated (*see Chapter 20, Interrupting Discussion — Procedural Motions, page 101, and Chapter 21, Interrupting Discussion — Demands, page 109*). All remarks must be addressed to the Chair.

Rule 19.1   Discussion

Characteristics:

Discussion at a society gathering

- can only take place on a debatable motion or amendment (*see chart, inside front cover*);

- is carried on under the supervision of the Chair in accordance with rules of order;

- must be relevant to the subject, impersonal, and always directed to the Chair;

- (if it concerns an amendment), must be limited to the amendment (the merits of the motion are not to be discussed);

Every person having the right to vote has an inherent right to enter into the discussion (unless he is ruled out of order and loses the floor, *see Rule 19.3, The Floor*). This right may be superseded only by another member who desires to make a motion or a demand which has a higher order of precedence than the motion or demand under discussion (*see chart, inside front cover*).

If the speaker fails to adhere strictly to the subject under discussion in a courteous, expeditious manner, or otherwise violates the rules of order, he shall be warned. If he persists, the Chair shall rule him out of order and he will lose the floor (*Rule 19.3*).

Rule 19.2   Opening the Discussion

Only the mover of a motion (or amendment) may speak to the motion (or amendment) before it has been seconded. Discussion shall not commence until the motion (or amendment) has been properly moved, seconded, and stated by the Chair. Before stating the question, the Chair must decide its validity and relevancy. In stating the question, the Chair repeats the motion and invites discussion.

In small meetings, the subject may be discussed before it is put in the form of a motion, and the motion is then formulated to conform with the sense of the meeting.

98

Rule 19.3   The Floor

A member who wishes to speak raises his hand or otherwise conveys to the Chair his desire to speak, but does not speak until recognized by the Chair. When recognized, he has the floor and may stand and speak. (In smaller meetings, where all of the members can sit around a table, it is not customary for a speaker to stand.)

If several voters request the floor simultaneously, the Chair determines the order in which they are to speak.

From a practical viewpoint, priority should be given to a member who has not yet spoken, or to one who is likely to have a view opposite to that of the previous speaker.

If the Chair rules a speaker out of order, the speaker shall lose the floor, discontinue speaking, and take his seat.

A speaker shall yield the floor temporarily for any motion or demand for which the speaker may be interrupted. (*See Chapter 20, Interrupting Discussion — Procedural Motions, page 101, and Chapter 21, Interrupting Discussion — Demands, page 109. See also chart, inside front cover.*) If he wishes to retain the floor, he should remain standing while the Chair deals with the interruption. If he sits, he loses his right to the floor, unless the Chair reserves it for him.

Rule 19.4   Speakers

Every member has the right to speak once on each motion and once on each amendment. With the consent of the meeting, every member, including the mover and the seconder, may be given another opportunity to speak.

The mover may speak a second time to explain his motion, answer questions, and close the discussion (reply) on his motion. He may not speak against the motion, but he may vote against it.

It is advisable for every speaker to indicate at the beginning and at the end of his statement whether he is "for" or "against" the motion or amendment (*see also Rule 19.2, above*).

Rule 19.5   Limiting the Time

The time allowed for discussion and length of speeches may be limited, within reason, by the Chair or by the meeting. However, the rights of minorities to be heard must not be suppressed. (*See Rule 20.5, Limiting Discussion, page 104, which allows the meeting to fix the length of speeches, the number of speeches, and the time to end discussion, and*

Rule 20.6, Voting Immediately, page 105, which allows the meeting to cease discussion and vote immediately (closure, guillotine).)

Rule 19.6   Closing the Discussion

When discussion has ended, or upon the moving and seconding of a non-debatable motion, the Chair shall call for a vote. He should be careful not to stifle debate. Everyone entitled to vote should be permitted to speak. If discussion has continued for a reasonable time, and viewpoints for and against have been given, the Chair may ask for a motion to terminate the discussion or vote immediately.

Form:

"All in favour of closing discussion, say 'Aye'. Any against, say 'No'."

CHAPTER 20

Interrupting Discussion — Procedural Motions

Rule 20.1 Objecting to Consideration

If a member feels that a main motion on the floor may be embarrassing, unnecessary, contrary to the society's policy, inopportune, or unwise, he may object to consideration of the motion and move this motion. If this motion is passed, discussion on the main motion ceases. This motion has all the characteristics of a demand, except that it requires a vote.

The Chair may either

(a) rule the motion out of order, or

(b) ask the meeting:

"Do you wish to have Item [*number*] deleted from the agenda?"

Note that the Chair poses his question in a positive manner, even if the motion is proposed negatively (see (ii), below).

(i) *Characteristics of a Motion to Object to Consideration*

- allows the speaker and the discussion to be interrupted in order to move this motion;

- must be moved as soon as the original motion is accepted by the Chair, or during the mover's introduction, before discussion has commenced. Once a second speaker begins, a motion to object to consideration cannot be proposed;

101

- takes precedence over all motions except closing motions and quorum count;

- does not require seconding, as it is a demand (*Chapter 21, Interrupting Discussion — Demands, page 109*) rather than a motion;

- is not open for discussion; rather, the motion (demand) must be voted on immediately;

- requires a two-thirds vote (because it suppresses discussion).

(ii) *Forms*

"I request that Item [*number*] not be considered at this meeting for the following reasons": [*reasons*].

"I object to consideration of this motion for the following reasons": [*reasons*].

Rule 20.2   Tabling Motions

A motion to table the main motion under discussion temporarily postpones the making of a decision until later at the same meeting or at the same conference. This motion closes discussion on the main motion and postpones the vote.

When the main motion is resumed, the mover of a motion to table has the first right to reopen the discussion, followed by members who have not spoken on it.

(i) *Characteristics of a Motion to Table a Motion*

- cannot be moved by anyone who has already spoken on the main motion;

- does not allow the speaker to be interrupted in order to move this motion;

- allows the discussion to be interrupted;

- requires seconding;

- is not amendable except as to time for resumption of main motion;

- must be voted on immediately;

- requires a two-thirds majority (because it suppresses discussion).

The main motion may be resumed by the Chair after all other business has been concluded or by any member on a motion to reopen.

(ii) *Motions*

> "I move that consideration of the motion to . . . be tabled until [*date or event*]", *or*
>
> "I move that this meeting adjourn until [*date and time*] and the discussion on the motion on the floor be tabled until the meeting reconvenes."

To reopen:

> "I move that the motion to . . . be now considered."

Rule 20.3   Postponing Discussion (To a Fixed Time)

A motion to postpone discussion is similar to a motion to table (*Rule 20.2*) except that the time referred to is at a future meeting.

Rule 20.4   Postponing Discussion Indefinitely

A motion to postpone discussion indefinitely is similar to a motion to table (*Rule 20.2*) except that no time or date is fixed for resumption of discussion. This motion has the same effect and characteristics as a motion to shelve, or to proceed to the next business. It is equivalent to a negative vote on the main motion without having it voted upon. The main motion may be renewed at any future meeting.

This is a motion that permits everyone to air his/her views on the subject, but avoids the necessity of the society going on record with a decision.

(i) *Characteristics of a Motion to Postpone Discussion Indefinitely*

- has the lowest order of precedence of all procedural motions;
- cannot be moved by anyone who has already spoken on the main motion;
- can only be applied with a motion to withdraw;
- does not allow the speaker to be interrupted in order to move this motion;
- allows the discussion to be interrupted;
- requires seconding;
- is not amendable;
- requires a two-thirds majority (because it suppresses discussion);

- cannot be brought up again during the same meeting or convention or adjournments. If it passes, it may be reconsidered. (*Rules 25.2, Reconsidering a Resolution, page 135; 25.3, Rescinding a Resolution, page 136; 25.4, Making a Resolution Unanimous, page 137.*)

(ii) *Motions*

"I move that the motion to . . . be postponed indefinitely", *or*

"That further discussion on this motion be postponed indefinitely", *or*

"That the meeting proceed to the next order of business", *or*

"That this motion be shelved."

Rule 20.5   Limiting Discussion

A motion to limit discussion permits the meeting to allocate time for each item of business on the agenda. It may be used to control the number and length of speeches, and to fix the time for ending the discussion. Because it may prevent some members from speaking on it, it must be used with caution. The motion may be moved either at the beginning of or during the debate.

Before a motion to limit discussion is voted upon, the Chair should explain that a "Yes" vote on this motion is not a vote in favour of or against the main motion. It is merely a vote on a motion to limit or restrict discussion. A "No" vote continues discussion unrestrictedly.

(i) *Characteristics of a Motion to Limit Discussion*

- cannot be moved by anyone who has spoken on the main motion;
- takes precedence over all other procedural motions;
- can have no motions applied to it except a motion to withdraw, or a motion to amend as to the length of the speeches, the number of speeches, and the time to cut off discussion;
- in order to move this motion, a member speaking (on another matter) may not be interrupted, but the discussion may be interrupted before another speaker is given the floor;
- is not amendable except as to the length of speeches, the number of speeches, and the time to cut off discussion;
- requires a two-thirds majority (because it suppresses discussion);
- if defeated, can be reviewed after other speeches have intervened.

104

(ii) *Motions*

"That discussion on the motion be limited to [*number*] members."

"That discussion on the motion be limited to not more than [*number*] minutes per speech."

"That discussion on this motion be closed at [*time*] and a vote be taken immediately thereafter."

Any two or three of these motions may be combined.

Rule 20.6 Voting Immediately

A motion to vote immediately or to close discussion (or closure, guillotine), if carried, stops all discussion, prevents additional amendments from being attached to the main motion, and brings the motion to an immediate vote. This motion is a device for securing a speedy decision. If this motion is carried, the main motion is put to a vote without further discussion. If it is defeated, discussion continues.

This motion is a successor to the "question" motions ("put the question", "next question", etc.), the meaning, procedure, and authority of which differ in the U.S. and in Great Britain. There does not appear to be any unanimity on whether the passage of a question motion closes discussion on the main motion or calls for a vote.

The Chair is not obligated to accept this motion if it feels that the views of the minority have not been fully aired. The Chair may declare discussion closed and call for an immediate vote without a motion when it appears that all views have been stated and the meeting acquiesces to closure. (*See Rule 19.6, Closing the Discussion, page 100.*)

Before a motion to vote immediately is voted upon, the Chair should explain that a "Yes" vote on this motion is not a vote in favour of or against the main motion. It is merely a vote to stop discussion and proceed to a vote. A "No" vote continues discussion.

(i) *Characteristics of a Motion to Vote Immediately*

- cannot be moved by anyone who has spoken on the main motion;
- takes precedence over all other procedural motions;
- can be applied to all debatable motions and can have no motions applied to it except a motion to withdraw;
- does not allow the speaker to be interrupted (because there is no urgency);

105

- allows the discussion to be interrupted in order to move this motion;
- requires seconding;
- is not amendable;
- is not debatable;
- requires a two-thirds majority (because it suppresses discussion);
- if defeated, can be renewed after other speeches have intervened, or allows a motion to limit discussion (*Rule 20.5*) to be moved.

(ii) *Motions*

"I move that a vote be taken immediately."

"I move that discussion close and that a vote be taken immediately."

(*See also Chapter 21, Interrupting Discussion — Demands, page 109.*)

Rule 20.7   Referring or Referring Back

A motion to refer, if carried, refers the question to the board or a committee for consideration or reconsideration and report. This motion may have attached to it an appointment of a committee. If it is a motion that the board or a committee has already considered, it is a motion to refer back.

It may be used as a means of deferring consideration on the main motion for the time being. It may also be used to have the main motion considered by a smaller group, which might give it a more thorough consideration, especially if the subject-matter is complex.

(i) *Characteristics of a Motion to Refer or Refer Back*

- does not allow the speaker to be interrupted to move this motion;
- allows the discussion to be interrupted to move this motion;
- requires seconding;
- is amendable only as to the items referred to the board or committee (terms of reference);
- has no precedence except over the main motion and amendments, and applies only to main motions;
- allows only motions to withdraw (*Rule 17.10, Withdrawing a Motion, page 89*) or motions to vote immediately (*Rule 20.6*) to be applied to it;

- may have added to it the appointment of a committee to consider it and refer back;
- is debatable only as to the propriety of referring the motion (back) to the board or to an existing committee or to a new committee;
- requires a two-thirds majority.

(ii) *Motions*

"That the [*main*] motion be referred to the board for consideration and that the board report back to the members at its next meeting."

"That the [*main*] motion be referred to and that the [*type*] committee report back to the members at its next meeting."

"That the [*main*] motion be referred to a committee comprised of A, B, and C for consideration and that this committee report back to the members at its meeting on [*date*]."

(*See also Rule 9.1, Resolving into Committee of the Whole, page 37, and Rule 9.2, Suspending the Rules, page 39.*)

CHAPTER 21

Interrupting Discussion — Demands

Rule 21.1 Demands

A demand is a request made to the Chair to assert a parliamentary right. It requires the immediate attention of the Chair, even if a speaker has the floor when the demand is made.

However, the meeting must not be interrupted merely to contradict or explain something to the Chair or a speaker. This should wait until the speaker or the discussion has concluded.

The discussion and the speaker having the floor may be interrupted for demands.

Demands (sometimes erroneously called "appeals") do not require seconding and do not need to be voted on.

If the Chair concurs with the demand, he will take the appropriate action; if he does not, his ruling may be appealed to the meeting (*Rule 10.9, Appeals from Rulings of the Chair, page 49*).

If the Chair refuses the demand, or if the demander is dissatisfied with the result, the demander may restate his demand as a motion.

Procedure:

The procedure for interrupting the discussion with a demand is as follows:

- the member must stand and demand the attention of the Chair,
- all proceedings cease until the demand is dealt with,

- the speaker must cease and resume his seat (he does not lose the floor),
- demands need not be seconded,
- demands are not debatable,
- demands take precedence over all motions except a call for a quorum count and closing motions.

Rule 21.2 Point of Personal Privilege

If a member has been subjected to insult or abuse, he may interrupt the meeting (*Rule 21.1*) to raise a point of personal privilege.

Procedure:

Without waiting to be recognized by the Chair, a member stands and says

"I have a request" *or*

"Point of personal privilege!"

The Chair will then ask him to explain his demand. If the Chair concurs, he will take the appropriate action; if he does not, his ruling may be appealed (*Rule 10.9, Appeals from Rulings of the Chair, page 49*).

Rule 21.3 Point of General Privilege

If there is any problem affecting the comfort or convenience of a member at a meeting, or if (a) a member finds it difficult to hear or be heard because of excessive background noise or poor acoustics, (b) the lighting is poor, or (c) the seating is inadequate, or if there is any other difficulty which makes the members physically uncomfortable, a member may interrupt the meeting (*Rule 21.1*) to raise a point of general privilege.

Procedure:

Without waiting to be recognized by the Chair, a member stands and says

"I have a request" *or*

"Point of general privilege!"

The Chair will then ask him to explain his point of general privilege. If the Chair concurs, he will take the appropriate action; if he does not, his ruling may be appealed (*Rule 10.9, Appeals from Rulings of the Chair, page 49*).

Rule 21.4 Point of Information

Members have the right to have all the information necessary for the understanding of the motion under discussion. They may interrupt the proceedings in order to be read the motion and all the technical and statistical data and background relating thereto. A member may interrupt the meeting (*Rule 21.1*) to raise a point of information. The request must be made in good faith and must not be argumentative or challenging.

Procedure:

Without waiting to be recognized by the Chair, a member stands and says

"Request" *or*

"I have a request" *or*

"I have a point of information" *or*

"Point of information!" *or*

"May I ask a question on a point of information?"

The Chair will then ask him what information he requires, whereupon the member will respond

"We need to know . . ." *or*

"We weren't told how much . . . etc."

If the Chair agrees that the information requested is relevant and ought to be made available, he complies. If the member is not satisfied with the Chair's ruling, he may appeal (*Rule 10.9, Appeals from Rulings of the Chair, page 49*).

Rule 21.5 Point of Procedure
(Parliamentary Inquiry)

Members have the right to interrupt a meeting (*Rule 21.1*) in order to ask the Chair, or a speaker having the floor, questions regarding the parliamentary procedure that is being followed or that is about to be followed, or the result of such procedure in respect of the motion under discussion. The question or request must be made in good faith and must not be argumentative or challenging.

Procedure:

Without waiting to be recognized by the Chair, a member stands and says

"Request! Point of procedure!" *or*

"Point of parliamentary inquiry!"

"Can this motion be amended? Is a motion to adjourn in order?"

If the Chair agrees that the question is relevant and ought to be answered, he complies. If the member is not satisfied with the Chair's ruling, he may appeal (*Rule 10.9, Appeals from Rulings of the Chair, page 49*).

Rule 21.6 Point of Order

Members have the right to interrupt a meeting (*Rule 21.1*) in order to draw to the attention of the Chair some irregularity in the proceedings (e.g., the rules of order are being violated, the agenda is not being followed, or the time for the special order has arrived (*Rule 13.6, Special Order, page 68*)). A point of order may be raised at any time during the meeting.

Procedure:

Without waiting to be recognized by the Chair, a member stands and says

"Request! Point of order! These proceedings are not in conformance with our constitution (or with a previous decision of this meeting). The time for the special order has arrived."

Rule 21.7 Correcting an Error

Members have the right to interrupt a meeting for the purpose of correcting an error made by the Chair or a previous speaker, or to correct any misconceptions that may develop at the meeting.

Procedure:

Without waiting to be recognized by the Chair, a member stands and says

"Request! I wish to correct an error made by Mr. A"

The Chair will ask him to explain his point.

"Mr. A stated that . . . , but the fact is that . . . ."

If the Chair agrees that an error exists, he will make the corrections. If he disagrees, he will proceed with the meeting.

If the member is not satisfied with the Chair's ruling, he may appeal (*Rule 10.9, Appeals from Rulings of the Chair, page 49*).

See also Rule 20.1, Objecting to Consideration, page 101.

¶ 2180   Quorum Count

For demand of quorum count, see Rule 15.2, Quorum Count (Attendance), page 74.

CHAPTER 22

Voting Methods

¶ 2200   Introduction

It is the duty of the Chair to ascertain the sense of the meeting with regard to all questions properly brought before it, and to decide all questions in accordance with the voting methods established by the constitution (*see Chapter 4, Voting Systems, page 13*).

Most motions dealt with at meetings of societies are passed without a poll being taken. There are several quick though imprecise methods of getting the sense of the meeting:

1. voice vote (*Rule 22.3*)

2. acquiescence (*Rule 22.4*)

3. show of hands (*Rule 22.5*)

These methods rely upon the tacit approval of the members. If any one member demands a poll (precise count), the Chair is obliged to concur. These methods are only used when there is little doubt as to the probable result of the vote. They must not be used where a special or extraordinary resolution is required (*Rule 23.1, Voting — Majorities,*

115

page 124), unless the opposition is non-existent or so minimal that the required approval is a foregone conclusion.

More precise methods of counting votes are as follows:

1. show of hands (*Rule 22.7*), followed by a count of uplifted hands;

2. division (*Rule 22.8*);

3. roll call (*Rule 22.9*);

4. ballot (*Rule 22.10*);

5. telephone, electronic devices (*Rule 22.11*).

There is no secret vote unless the constitution expressly provides for it. Every member is entitled to know (a) how every other member voted, and (b) that each member was qualified to vote on that motion or election.

Rule 22.1 Right to Vote

Every member, provided that he is qualified under the constitution to vote on a particular issue, has the right to vote or to abstain from voting, as he wishes.

A member at a meeting of members may vote as he pleases regardless of his personal interest or the possible consequences of the vote, provided that he is not disqualified from voting and that no fraud is committed against the minority in consequence of the vote. The courts will not invalidate a member's vote merely because he has a personal interest in the subject matter different from or opposed to that of the society.

Rule 22.2 No Obligation to Vote

Neither the mover nor the seconder of a motion is obliged to vote on the motion. They may refrain from voting, no matter what the reason or the result. It is undemocratic to compel a member to vote.

Quick Voting Methods

Rule 22.3 Voice Vote. A vote by voice is a simple and quick method of voting, but it is not conclusive. It is an imperfect method of voting and is not recommended except where the vote is unquestionably one-sided (practically unanimous), as in an acclamation. The Chair makes his decision on the volume of sound as he perceives it. If there is any doubt as to the outcome, the Chair or any member may ask for a poll to be taken, provided this request is made immediately.

Procedure:

The procedure for voting by voice is as follows:

"All in favour, say 'Aye',"

"All in favour, please applaud."

"All opposed, say 'Nay',"

"All opposed, please applaud."

Rule 22.4 Acquiescence (Consensus). In the case of routine, non-controversial questions, if the Chair feels that the meeting is unanimous in its opinion, and if there is no objection, he may assume that the members approve of his action or statement. If any objection is voiced, the Chair must call for a poll.

Procedure:

The procedure for voting by acquiescence is as follows:

"Is everyone ready for the question?"

"Are there any corrections (to the minutes)? Hearing none, the minutes will stand verified as read."

"If no one objects, we will proceed with the meeting."

"If no one objects, we will consider the matter approved (*or* rejected)."

Rule 22.5 Show of Hands. A vote by a show of hands is also a quick but imperfect method of voting, unless the Chair counts the upraised hands.

(i) *Procedure*

The procedure for voting by a show of hands is as follows:

"All in favour, please raise one hand . . ."

"All against, please raise one hand . . ."

If a poll is not demanded (*Rule 22.6, Demand for a Poll*), and the Chair declares the result, it is conclusive. If there is any doubt as to the outcome, the Chair or any member may ask for a poll to be taken.

"All in favour, please raise one hand"
(a count is taken),

"Any opposed, please raise one hand, but not if you have already voted"
(a count is taken).

(ii) *Stand-up Vote*

This is the same as a vote by a show of hands and may be more accurate. The procedure is as follows:

"All in favour, please stand up"
(a count is taken),

"Please be seated."

"All opposed, please stand up"
(a count is taken),

"Please be seated."

Precise Count

Rule 22.6 Demand for a Poll.

(i) *Demand*

The Chair or any member may demand a poll on any motion before, during, or immediately after a vote by any of the quick voting methods (*Rules 22.3, 22.4, 22.5*). The Chair shall then decide which of the polling methods is to be adopted:

- show of hands with count (*Rule 22.7*)
- division (*Rule 22.8*)
- roll call (*Rule 22.9*)
- ballot (*Rule 22.10*)
- telephone or electronics (*Rule 22.11*)

Whichever method is adopted, the poll must be taken immediately, but in certain circumstances (*Rule 23.9, Recounts and Revotes, page 125*), the result need not be declared immediately.

(ii) *Withdrawal*

Once a poll has been demanded, it cannot be withdrawn without the consent of the meeting.

(iii) *Previous Vote*

Once a poll has been demanded, all previous votes (by voice, acquiescence, or show of hands) are negated.

(iv) *Specific Majority*

If the constitution requires a specific majority to pass a motion (for a special or extraordinary resolution), a poll should be taken, unless it is obvious that the opposition is minimal.

(v) *Demand by Proxyholder*

Where proxies are permitted, a proxyholder is not qualified to demand a poll unless authority to do so is given in the proxy in specific or general terms.

Rule 22.7 Show of Hands With Count. A show of hands constitutes a poll if a count is taken (*see Rule 22.5*).

On a show of hands, if a count is taken, only the members who are present and voting are counted. Where proxies are allowed, proxyholders may vote only for themselves (if they have a vote), not for the absent members who appointed them.

Rule 22.8 Division. Voting by division is done by separating the members into separate groups — those in favour of the motion going into one room, and those against going into another room or hall. One group may be asked to remain in the meeting room. The members in each room are counted and the Chair declares the result.

On a vote by division, a person holding a proxy has only one vote (if he is entitled to vote in his own right). He is not entitled to vote on behalf of his appointors.

Rule 22.9 Roll Call. The names of all members are read out in order, and the member is asked to respond by declaring his vote (Aye, Yes, No, Nay, For, Against). The Chair (with the help of the scrutineers, if there are any) tabulates and declares the result.

As an alternative, the members may be asked to give their names to a scrutineer collecting affirmative votes (Aye) or to another scrutineer collecting negative votes (Nay).

On a vote by roll call, a person holding a proxy may vote for himself only, as in the case of a division (*Rule 22.8*).

Rule 22.10 Balloting.

(i) *Procedure*

The procedure for balloting is as follows:

1. A ballot is handed to every member entitled to vote. The paper may either be blank or imprinted with "For" and "Against" and a line for signature.

2. If the paper is blank, the voter writes "For" or "Against", or "Yes" or "No" on it and signs it legibly. If it does not clearly indicate the intentions of the voter, it may be disallowed.

3. If the member is voting as a proxy, he must indicate that fact on the ballot. If he does not do so, he will not be counted. He must vote in accordance with his instructions, if any, on the proxy; otherwise the ballot may be disallowed.

4. The Chair collects and examines all ballots, decides on their validity, counts the votes cast, and declares the result (*Rule 22.12*).

(ii) *Scrutineers*

The Chair may delegate to scrutineers (*Rule 16.7, Meeting Duly Constituted, page 79*) the examination of the ballots, the consideration of their validity, and the counting. He may adopt or reject the scrutineers' report in whole or in part.

(iii) *Possession of Ballots*

When ballots (and proxies) are deposited with the society, they become records of the society. The Chair, the scrutineers and the members may examine them at any reasonable time, during or after the meeting.

Adequate precautions should be taken to prevent any tampering with or disappearance of ballots, proxies, ballot papers, and scrutineers' summaries, so long as the possibility of controversy exists. A motion to destroy the ballots after a reasonable period is sometimes acceptable, especially if no controversy is anticipated. (*See also Rule 14.7, Possession of Proxies, page 71.*)

Rule 22.11 Telephone or Electronics. If permitted by the constitution, a vote may be recorded by telephone, telegraph, telex, fax, or other electronic means.

It is the responsibility of the Chair to ensure that the sender of the vote (by telegraph, telex, or fax) or the speaker on the telephone is a member entitled to vote. For this purpose the Chair may enlist the assistance of scrutineers to assist him in the verification. Such verification may be done by telephone or any other reliable medium.

Rule 22.12 Chair's Decision

A declaration by the Chair that a motion has been carried or defeated, or that a certain person(s) has/have been elected or appointed, (and an entry to that effect made in the minutes of the meeting), constitutes prima facie evidence of the fact without proof of the number or proportion of the votes recorded in favour of or against the resolution. The Chair's decision stands unless reversed by the members or the court. (*See Chapter 23, Sense of the Meeting, page 123.*)

Rule 22.13 Timing for Chair's Decision

If the poll is on the election of a Chair or on any closing motion, the votes shall be counted immediately and the result shall be declared before any further business is conducted. On any other question, the count shall commence immediately, but other business may be proceeded with pending the completion of the count.

See Rule 10.9, Appeals from Rulings of the Chair, page 49.

CHAPTER 23

Sense of the Meeting

¶ 2300   Introduction

It is the duty of the Chair to ascertain the sense of the meeting with regard to all questions properly brought before it, and to declare the result (*see Chapter 10, The Chair, page 43*).

The basic simple majority (more votes cast *for* than *against*) has always been and still is the rule for all parliamentary bodies in Canada (e.g., the House of Commons in Ottawa, and the provincial legislatures), as well as for corporations and societies incorporated under Canadian law. However, Canadian corporation law and practice has also developed the concept of special majorities (higher than a simple majority) for certain types of motions involving fundamental changes to a corporation or restrictions on the rights of the minority at a meeting (see "Procedural Motions" on chart, inside front cover). In the United States, unlike Canada and Great Britain, there is a parliamentary tradition of special majorities that is enshrined in the Constitution.

If the meeting is duly convened, and a proper resolution is duly passed by the required majority (*Rule 23.1*), the vote is binding on the minority and on those who did not vote or who voted against it.

Rule 23.1 Voting — Majorities

Unless otherwise provided in the constitution (*see Glossary, page xvii*),

(a) ordinary questions are decided by a simple majority vote of the persons actually voting (more votes are cast *for* than *against*);

(b) special questions, such as changing the constitution or the bylaws, dissolving the society, etc., are decided by a two-thirds majority vote (two-thirds of the votes cast are in favour of the motion, and abstentions and spoiled ballots are not counted; for example, if there are fifty members present, and two are voting *for*, one is voting *against*, and forty-seven have abstained or have spoiled their ballots, the motion is carried by a two-thirds majority);

(c) motions involving restrictions on the rights of the minority at a meeting (for example, a motion to "object to consideration" of another motion, or a motion to vote immediately or limit discussion on a motion) require a two-thirds majority vote.

Under some constitutions, extraordinary questions require a greater than two-thirds vote — from 75 percent up to 100 percent.

The right of the majority of members to control the action of the meeting cannot be questioned.

Rule 23.2 Majority of Quorum

Where the constitution provides for a variable quorum for meetings, depending on the current number of members in good standing (a certain percentage of the membership), the meeting may require votes by a majority of the quorum to pass a resolution. Abstentions and blank or spoiled ballots are counted as if they were votes against the resolution.

Rule 23.3 Majority of Members Present

Where the constitution provides for the vote of a majority of members present to pass a resolution, abstentions and blank or spoiled ballots are counted as if they were votes against the resolution.

Rule 23.4 Majority of Membership

Where the constitution provides for the vote of a majority of the membership to pass a resolution, abstentions and blank or spoiled ballots are counted as if they were votes against the resolution.

Rule 23.5 Unanimous Vote

Where the constitution requires a unanimous vote to pass a resolution, one vote against it defeats the motion, but an abstention or spoiled ballot does not.

Rule 23.6 Tie Vote

A tie vote defeats the motion (*see Rule 10.8, Chair's Rights at Meetings, page 48*).

Rule 23.7 Open Voting

Unless the constitution provides otherwise, every member has the right to know how every other member voted and the exact count of the poll.

Rule 23.8 Changing a Vote

A member has the right to change his vote by voice, acquiescence, or show of hands up to the time the result is declared by the Chair. (Even after the result is declared, a member may demand a poll, and on the poll he may vote differently than he did on the "quick" vote — *see Rule 22.7, Show of Hands With Count, page 119*). A vote by ballot may be changed up to the time it reaches the Chair, the secretary, or the scrutineer.

Rule 23.9 Recounts and Revotes

Any person who votes on a motion may, immediately after the result is declared, request a recount or revote on the ground that the count was improper, or that the instructions were confusing, or that there were an abnormal number of spoiled ballots.

The procedure for requesting a recount or revote is as follows:

1. Voter:
   "I ask for a recount" [*or* revote].
2. Chair:
   "What is the basis for your request?"
3. Voter gives his reasons.
4. Chair rules on the request.
5. Voter has the right to appeal the ruling:
   "I appeal the Chair's ruling" (*see Rule 10.9, Appeals from Rulings of the Chair, page 49*).

6. Chair then asks the meeting or a voter to determine the issue by making a motion in a positive form:

"Resolved, That the ruling of the Chair be upheld."

This motion must be dealt with immediately. It does not require seconding. Furthermore, it is not debatable, but the appellant may give his reasons for the appeal, and the Chair may reply (*see Rule 10.9, Appeals from Rulings of the Chair, page 49*).

CHAPTER 24

Elections and Appointments

Elections

¶ 2400 **Introduction.** An election is the act of choosing freely from a number of persons to fill one or more positions, in contrast to an appointment, which is the act of selecting (*or* rejecting) a number of persons to fill one or more positions.

The constitution will determine whether the position(s) is/are to be filled by election (*Rules 24.4, Single Choice Elections, or 24.5, Multiple Choice Elections*) or by appointment (*Rule 24.7, Appointments*). Whether the constitution of the society is based upon the direct or the indirect organization model (*Chapter 3, Bylaws, page 11, and Chapter 5, Members, page 15*), the procedures are the same. In the former, the members elect the officers, and in the latter, the members elect the directors, who in turn elect the officers.

Rule 24.1 Nominations. A nomination is the act of proposing for election an individual to fill an office. Subject to some other procedure set out in the constitution, every member entitled to vote may nominate the number of candidates required to fill the number of offices to be filled. Unless the constitution states otherwise, nominations do not require seconding. They are not debatable or amendable.

Procedure:

The procedure for nominating an individual is as follows:

Chair:

> "The meeting is open for the election of [*number*] directors to constitute the board," *or*

> "The meeting is open for the election of [*number*] delegates to attend the conference on behalf of the society." (*See also Rule 24.7, below.*)

Member:

> "I nominate A, B, C, D, and E as directors," *or*

> "I nominate F as one of the directors."

Subject to specific provisions in the constitution, nominations may be made by

(a) any member from the floor (some constitutions require nominations to be seconded or to be made by two or three members);

(b) a nominating committee — *see Rule 24.3* (some constitutions permit both (a) and (b));

(c) advancement (e.g., a vice-president may automatically be nominated for president if the constitution provides for advancement);

(d) volunteering (there is nothing improper in volunteering to serve on a board or committee).

Rule 24.2 Closing Nominations. Nominations may be closed by the Chair (after a reasonable time has elapsed) or by resolution of the meeting. A speaker may not be interrupted for this motion.

Procedure:

A motion to close nominations requires seconding and is not debatable. A simple majority vote is sufficient. The procedure for closing a nomination is as follows:

Chair:

> "Are there any more nominations?"

Motion:

> "I move that nominations be closed."

Chair:

> "Before consideration of this motion, are there any more nominations? . . . All in favour? . . . All against? . . . Motion carried, we will now proceed with the elections." (*Continue as in Rule 24.4, Single Choice Elections, or Rule 24.5, Multiple Choice Elections.*)

Rule 24.3 Nominating Committee. The function of a nominating committee is to seek out members for office and to nominate them.

The nominating committee may be a standing committee (*Rule 8.2, Standing Committees, page 32*) created by the constitution, or a special committee (*Rule 8.3, Special Committees, page 33*) created each year by the members.

Unless the constitution provides otherwise, the committee may nominate more than one member for some offices, and leave the final selection to the members.

The nominating committee may nominate a complete slate (a member for each office), or it may nominate an incomplete slate and allow the members to fill in the vacancies from the floor.

The ideal nominating committee consists of four to six members, including

- a member with experience in the society, a past president, or a long-time member;
- a member of the executive;
- one or more ordinary members;
- a newcomer to the society.

It should not include any employee of the society.

Rule 24.4 Single Choice Elections. In an election to select one person (a single choice election), each member may cast one vote for the candidate of his choice. The selection may be by a plurality or a majority system of voting.

In the plurality system, the candidate receiving the highest number of votes is declared elected even though he may have received fewer than fifty percent of the votes cast. This is the most common system in use.

In the majority system, the first candidate receiving more than fifty percent of the votes cast is declared elected. This system is used in all political conventions for electing a party leader.

Until a candidate is declared elected, a number of "run-off" elections are held. For example, if no candidate receives fifty percent of the votes cast on the first ballot, the candidate receiving the lowest number of votes retires and another fresh vote is taken. If a candidate receives more than fifty percent of the votes cast, he is declared elected. However, if no candidate receives fifty percent of the votes cast, the candidate receiving the lowest number of votes retires and another fresh vote is taken. This is repeated until one candidate receives more than fifty percent of the votes and he is declared elected.

Sometimes a candidate may, before the election or after being defeated, indicate his preference for another candidate; however, his supporters are not obligated to vote for that person unless the constitution provides for transferable voting. This system is not considered democratic, as every member has the right to vote for or not to vote for any specific candidate.

Rule 24.5 Multiple Choice Elections. If there are more than two candidates to be selected for two or more identical positions (e.g., directors for the board of directors), the constitution may provide for one or more of the following voting methods:

(i) *Basic Method*

Most constitutions permit a voter to cast a single vote for his one favourite candidate, or to cast one vote for *each* of his several favourite candidates, up to the total number of vacancies to be filled. This is called the "*basic method*". (Of course, the voter always has the option of not voting at all.)

(ii) *Cumulative Voting*

If cumulative voting is authorized by the constitution, a member may cast more than one vote (or all of his votes) in favour of each of the candidates of his choice (or in favour of a single candidate). The total number of votes cast must not exceed the number of vacancies to be filled.

Casting all of your votes in favour of one candidate is called "plumping".

(iii) *Ranking Method*

If the ranking method of voting is required by the constitution, a member casts his votes in order of preference:

1. The member puts the number "1" beside the name of the candidate of his first choice.
2. The member puts the number "2" beside the name of the candidate of his second choice, and so on.

After the rankings on all ballots are tallied, the candidate with the lowest total is declared elected, and if more than one vacancy is being filled, the candidate with the second lowest total is declared elected, and so on until all vacancies are filled. The ballot must contain a different ranking for every candidate; if it does not, it must be treated as a spoiled ballot.

Procedure:

If more than the required number of candidates are nominated, a poll is taken as follows:

1. The Chair or the meeting may appoint scrutineers (*Rules 16.9, Appointment of Scrutineers; 16.10, Duties of Scrutineers, page 80*) to assist the Chair in collecting, examining, and counting the votes.

2. The Chair explains the method of voting to be used as required under the constitution:

   - basic (*Rule 24.5(i)*);

   - cumulative (*Rule 24.5(ii)*);

   - ranking (*Rule 24.5(iii)*);

3. A ballot is handed to every member entitled to vote. It may be imprinted with the names of all persons nominated, or it may be blank. If it is a blank ballot, the members are instructed to write the names of the candidates of their choice.

4. The ballot must be clearly marked to indicate the intention of the voter, and it must be legibly signed. (If the voter's usual signature is illegible, he should print his name below his signature.) If the voter has a membership number, he should put it on the ballot (although this is not essential for the validity of the ballot).

5. If a proxyholder is casting a vote on behalf of the person appointing him, the proxyholder must indicate this on the ballot and must give the name of the appointor; otherwise, the vote will not be counted. The Chair should instruct proxyholders to add to the ballot the words

   "on behalf of [*name of appointor*] who appointed me his proxy," *or*

   "for self and [*names of appointors*] who appointed me their proxy," or words to the same effect.

6. A proxyholder must vote in accordance with any instructions given to him on the proxy; otherwise, his vote will not be counted.

7. If the basic voting method is used, the members are instructed to mark an "X" opposite the names of the candidates of their choice (not more than the number of vacancies to be filled).

8. If the cumulative voting method is used, the members are instructed to place one or more "X"'s opposite the name or names of the candidates of their choice (not more "X"'s than the number of vacancies to be filled).

9. If the ranking method is used, the members are instructed to put number "1" beside the name of the candidate of their first choice,

number "2" beside the name of the candidate of their second choice, and so on until all of the candidates have received a different ranking.

10. The Chair collects the ballots, examines them, decides their validity, and counts the votes cast. If scrutineers have been appointed, they will assist the Chair in collecting, examining, and counting the votes, but only the Chair may rule on the validity of the ballots (*Rule 10.9, Appeals from Rulings of the Chair, page 49*).

11. On the completion of the election, whether by acclamation, single ballot, or poll, the Chair declares the successful candidates duly elected to office.

Rule 24.6 Acclamations. If only the exact number (or fewer) of candidates required to fill the vacancies is nominated, and nominations are properly closed (*Rule 24.2, Closing Nominations*), the Chair may

(a) declare the persons nominated elected to the offices by acclamation;

(b) ask for a motion to declare the persons nominated elected to the offices by acclamation;

(c) ask for a motion to direct the secretary to cast, on behalf of all the members, a ballot in favour of the persons nominated for election.

(i) *Motions*

The motion to declare the persons nominated elected to the offices by acclamation

- requires seconding
- is not amendable
- requires only a simple majority

"I move that the persons nominated be declared elected to the offices named."

If the constitution requires a vote by ballot, the secretary or any other member may be authorized, on behalf of all the members, to cast a ballot in favour of the persons nominated for election. This motion

- requires seconding
- is not amendable
- requires only a simple majority

132

"I move that the secretary of the meeting is hereby authorized, on behalf of the members present, to cast a ballot for the election of the persons nominated to the offices named."

(ii) *Ballot*

"On behalf of the members present, I cast this ballot for the election of .... to the offices of .... respectively."

....
Secretary

Rule 24.7 Appointments

An appointment is the act of naming, as opposed to electing, a person to an office. There is no choice or selection, only the right to select or reject. A negative vote is a rejection. Some constitutions provide that all or some of the officers may be appointed instead of elected.

Where the constitution provides for the appointment of a person to a position, it is filled as follows:

1. The Chair calls for a motion to fill the position.

2. He receives a motion to appoint a qualified person to the position.

   Chair:

   "May I have a motion to appoint a [*secretary*] of the meeting?"

   Member:

   "I move that Mr. A be appointed [*secretary*] of the meeting."

3. The Chair deals with the motion in the usual manner. Anyone desiring the appointment of a different person may vote against the motion, and if the motion is defeated, he may move for the appointment of the candidate of his choice.

4. If the motion to appoint is carried, the Chair declares the person named appointed to that office. If the motion is defeated, the Chair requests another motion to appoint, naming another person and so on until a motion to appoint is carried.

As a variation to the above procedure, the Chair may request the members to suggest names. If only one name is proposed, he requests a motion to declare the named person appointed to the office. If more than one name is proposed, the meeting will vote on one at a time in the order in which they were proposed until one succeeds in obtaining a majority vote.

CHAPTER 25

Reviewing Resolutions and Motions

¶ 2500 Introduction

It sometimes happens that members have second thoughts about the wording or the wisdom of a resolution they passed or a motion they defeated. New information may have come to light, or new insights may have been gained through private discussion. A motion to reconsider is available for this purpose.

For dividing a motion on the floor, see Rule 17.9, Dividing a Motion, page 88. For withdrawing a motion on the floor, see Rule 17.10, Withdrawing a Motion, page 89.

Rule 25.1 Reconsidering a Defeated Motion

A motion to reconsider or renew a motion that has been defeated may be made only once. If passed, it cancels the vote on the original motion and reopens it for discussion.

In all other respects, the procedure is similar to Rule 25.2, below.

Rule 25.2 Reconsidering a Resolution

A motion to reconsider a resolution may be made at any time provided that no one has acted on it, and it can be reversed. Closing motions cannot be reconsidered.

A resolution cannot be reconsidered if it authorizes a payment to be made and that payment is made, or if it elected or appointed someone to an office and that person was present or was notified, or if it approved a contract and the other party was present or was notified.

If a motion to reconsider is passed, it cancels the vote and the resolution; the original motion is revived and the discussion on it is resumed.

A motion to reconsider may be moved by anyone, whether he voted for or against it, or did not vote at all.

(i) *Procedure*

A motion to reconsider a resolution

- does not allow the speaker or the discussion to be interrupted;
- requires seconding;
- is not amendable;
- is debatable, if the original motion was debatable;
- requires the same majority as the resolution which it seeks to have reconsidered;
- takes precedence over main motions (*see chart, inside front cover*);
- may have all motions applied to it except those which delay consideration;
- requires notice, if the original motion required notice;
- cannot be moved a second time.

(ii) *Motion*

"I move that the resolution to . . . that was passed earlier today [*or* on the . . .] be reconsidered."

Rule 25.3 Rescinding a Resolution

A motion to rescind a resolution is in all respects similar to the procedure in Rule 25.2.

A motion to expunge from the minutes may be added to the motion to rescind if the passage of the resolution is embarrassing or otherwise undesirable. A motion to expunge may be subsequently moved as a separate motion (*Rule 25.5*).

If a motion to rescind a resolution is passed, the original motion is deemed to have been defeated.

Motion:

"I move that the resolution to . . . that was passed earlier today be rescinded [*and that the same be expunged from the minutes*]."

Rule 25.4 Making a Resolution Unanimous

A motion to make a resolution unanimous, if passed, does not alter the vote on the original motion, but it superposes an additional result. It may be proposed only by a person who voted against the original motion. This motion is only symbolic and is used to display loyalty by the defeated side to the successful side. Therefore, it may be moved only by a person who voted against the motion. A defeated candidate for an office, or a member who led an opposition group (as in a proxy contest) may propose this motion as a show of good sportsmanship.

(i) *Procedure*

A motion to make the resolution unanimous

- does not allow the speaker or the discussion to be interrupted
- requires seconding
- is not amendable or debatable
- must be passed unanimously

(ii) *Motion*

"I move that the resolution [*or* appointment, *or* election] . . . be made unanimous."

Rule 25.5 Expunging from Minutes

If a resolution or defeated motion appearing in the minutes of a meeting is embarrassing or otherwise undesirable, all reference to it may be expunged by a motion to expunge.

The offensive minutes are crossed out and, in the margin, the following words are added:

"Expunged by the society on [date]."

No copies or extracts may be made from them.

(i) *Procedure*

The procedure for a motion to expunge is in all respects similar to the procedure in Rule 25.2.

(ii) *Motion*

"I move that all references to the resolution [*or* a motion to the resolution] . . . be expunged from the minutes."

CHAPTER 26

Closing the Meeting

¶ 2600   Introduction

Closing motions are motions to

- conclude the meeting (all business is completed);
- adjourn the meeting to a fixed date (*cum die*) or to an unfixed date (*sine die*) (to resume unfinished business on the date fixed or to be fixed);
- recess the meeting (to resume unfinished business on the same day).

Rule 26.1 Closing Motions

(i) *Characteristics*

A motion to close the meeting (conclude, adjourn, or recess)

- has the highest priority of all motions;
- applies to no other motion and can have no motion applied to it except a motion to withdraw (*Rule 17.10, Withdrawing a Motion, page 89*);
- if defeated, cannot be repeated until other business has intervened.

The Chair need not accept a closing motion if, in his opinion, it is an abuse of privilege or it is moved merely to obstruct business. It is the Chair's duty to continue the meeting until all its business has been concluded (*see Rule 26.2*). He should make every effort to continue the meeting.

139

(ii) Procedure

A motion to close the meeting

- is not amendable (except as to time and place of reconvening, where the motion is to adjourn or recess the meeting);

- allows the discussion to be interrupted, but not while a speaker has the floor;

- requires seconding;

- is not debatable (except as to time and place of reconvening, where the motion is to adjourn or recess the meeting);

- requires a simple majority;

- cannot be moved

  (a) when someone has the floor;

  (b) while a demand (*Chapter 21, Interrupting Discussion — Demands, page 109*) is being considered;

  (c) immediately after a similar motion has been defeated, unless other business has intervened;

  (d) when another version of a closing motion is on the floor;

  (e) while a vote is being taken or while ballots are being counted on a closing motion.

Rule 26.2 Concluding Meeting

A motion to conclude (when all business is finished), if passed, dissolves the meeting completely.

For procedure, see Rule 26.1(ii).

Rule 26.3 Adjourning Meeting to Fixed Date

A motion to adjourn to a fixed date suspends the meeting, to reconvene on the fixed date. It has no effect on the agenda. Unfinished business is taken up when the meeting reconvenes on the fixed date. A motion to adjourn has the highest precedence of any motion.

Motion:

"I move that this meeting adjourn, to reconvene on [*date*] at [*hour*] at [*place*]."

For procedure, see Rule 26.1(ii).

Rule 26.4 Adjourning Meeting Without Fixed Date

A motion to adjourn to an unfixed date, if passed, does not cancel out unfinished business. After the meeting is adjourned, the person or persons having authority to call meetings must give notice of the date, place, and time of the continuation of the adjourned meeting, unless the resolution adjourning the meeting delegates this function to someone else (e.g., the secretary). No new agenda is required for the continued meeting.

Motion:

"I move that this meeting be adjourned, and that the secretary arrange the date, place, and time of the continuation of the meeting and notify the members promptly."

For procedure, see Rule 26.1(ii).

Rule 26.5 Adjournment by the Chair

The Chair may, with the consent of the meeting, adjourn the meeting from time to time and from place to place according to such conditions as the meeting determines. The Chair has no power to close the meeting without the consent of the meeting except

- where discussion has degenerated and the transaction of business has become impossible,

- where a quorum is lacking, or

- when all the business of the meeting has been concluded.

If the Chair has properly adjourned the meeting, it cannot be continued by the members (*see Rule 26.7*).

Rule 26.6 Recessing Meeting

If the meeting becomes heated or out of control, or if the session is too long, a motion to recess may be appropriate.

This motion, if passed, suspends the meeting for a short time (not more than a couple of hours), to reconvene on the same day. It has no effect on the agenda. It takes precedence over all motions except other closing motions.

A break for coffee is well worth the time. It will ease any situation, and the resumed meeting will continue in a better, more relaxed atmosphere.

Note: The Chair should not vacate the chair (Rule 10.6, Vacating the Chair, page 48). If he must leave, he should appoint a temporary Chair (Rule 10.4, Temporary Chair, page 46).

Motion:

"I move that this meeting recess, to reconvene at [*time*]."

For procedure, see Rule 26.1(ii).

Rule 26.7 Improper Adjournment

If the Chair has improperly adjourned the meeting, vacated the chair, or disqualified himself by his actions, the meeting may be continued by the members, who shall elect another (substitute) Chair (*see Rule 10.5, Removal of Chair, page 47*).

The shareholder should pass a motion (with or without the help of the Chair) to adjourn and convene in the same or adjacent room either immediately or at a specified time within the hour.

Rule 26.8 Reconvened Meeting

The reconvened meeting is deemed to be a continuation of the meeting. Subject to Rule 26.7, the Chair who presided at the original meeting is entitled to preside at the reconvened meeting.

No new business not covered in the notice of the original meeting may be transacted unless a new and proper notice is given (*see Chapter 12, Notice of General Meetings, page 59*).

By participating in a reconvened meeting, the members are deemed to have waived any irregularity in the adjournment.

CHAPTER 27

Minutes of Meetings

¶ 2700   Introduction

Minutes are the official record of the deliberations that take place and the decisions that are made at meetings. A special book should be kept for this purpose; a large loose-leaf binder is ideal.

Once minutes have been verified by the members or by the board, or by a committee, as the case may be, and signed by the proper officer (usually the recording secretary and/or the Chair or the president), they must not be altered in any way (*see Rule 27.6*) without the prior approval of a meeting.

Minutes come in many forms: Rule 27.2 sets out the minimum requirements for minutes of general meetings, and lists additional matters that may be dealt with in the minutes. It is not necessary to keep verbatim minutes for either general meetings or board meetings. *For minutes of board and committee meetings, see Rule 27.2.*

Rule 27.1 Keeping the Minutes

The secretary is responsible for and must ensure that proper minutes are kept of all general meetings and board meetings. The secretary of each committee, or, if there is no committee secretary, the Chair of the committee, is responsible for minutes of committee meetings.

Rule 27.2 Contents of Minutes

The minutes of general meetings and board meetings must contain at least

- the date, time, and place of the meeting;
- a statement that a quorum was present, or a list of all members present, or both;
- a statement that proper notice was given (a copy of the notice with proof of mailing may be annexed);
- the motions that were passed (resolutions);
- other business that was transacted, or proposals that were adopted;
- the reports of officers and committees (in full, or summarized, or annexed), and an explanation of how they were dealt with.

The minutes of general meetings and board meetings may also contain

- the names of persons present;
- motions that were defeated;
- the names of movers and seconders of motions passed or defeated, the method of voting, and the count.

Minutes of committee meetings should be more detailed than minutes of members' or board meetings, since most committees make recommendations rather than final decisions, and recommendations without reasons are worthless to the decision-making body. A summary of the discussion should be included in the minutes, unless the viewpoints of the majority and of the minority of the committee members are reflected in the report(s) of the committee.

Form:

Formal, ritualistic language in minutes should be minimized. Instead of saying

"It was moved by John Smith, seconded by Jane Doe, and unanimously carried, that the meeting be concluded,"

it is preferable to use the following format:

"Moved/Seconded/Carried, That the meeting be concluded" *or*

"Moved (Smith)/Seconded (Doe)/Carried, That the meeting be concluded."

If the number of votes cast for and against is significant (e.g., if a special majority is required, or if the motion is highly contentious), the secretary should record the vote as follows:

"Moved (Smith)/Seconded (Doe)/Carried (50:35) (or if there are abstentions, (50:35:5) as the case may be)."

Rule 27.3 Signing the Minutes

Minutes, when written or typed, ought to be signed by the Chair and the secretary of the meeting. They may be signed at any time.

Unless the constitution provides otherwise, minutes need not be verified at a subsequent meeting.

Rule 27.4 Minutes as Evidence

When the minutes are signed, the meeting is deemed to have been duly called, constituted, and held. Unless and until refuted, such minutes and the resolutions therein set out are deemed to be true and accurate.

Minutes, whether signed or not, may be contradicted or proved by parol evidence of persons who were present at the meeting.

The passage of unrecorded resolutions may be proved by oral evidence of persons who were present at the meeting.

Unsigned minutes will not prevent their being used as evidence.

Rule 27.5 Verification of Minutes

The minutes of a previous meeting may be verified by the signature of the Chair or secretary of such meeting, or by the signature of the Chair or secretary of a subsequent meeting after a resolution to verify has been passed. Discussion on the business of the previous meeting is not in order on the motion to verify. Only the accuracy of the minutes may be discussed, except on a motion to reconsider a resolution passed at a previous meeting. There is no legal requirement to have minutes verified, but it is considered good practice. The motion does not by itself ratify or adopt the business transacted; it merely verifies the minutes as being correct.

To attend a subsequent meeting where minutes are read and verified as correct does not, by itself, make those who are present at the subsequent meeting responsible for what was done at the preceding meeting, unless they vote in favour of a further motion to carry out the resolution passed at the previous meeting or to adopt the resolution. The safest course for the person who does not wish to be liable is to raise an objection either at the meeting at which the original motion was passed, or at the subsequent meeting, and to insist that his objection be noted in the minutes.

Motions to verify may have added to them words for adoption and ratification.

(i) *Procedure*

The procedure to verify minutes of a previous meeting is as follows:

1. The Chair asks the members if they have received the minutes of the previous meeting, and if not, and the meeting wants them read, the secretary reads the minutes to the meeting. A motion to dispense with the reading may be passed.

2. The Chair asks for any errors or omissions. If there is no objection, he may sign the minutes. A declaration of the Chair to the effect that the minutes stand verified is sufficient.

3. If there are objections, the Chair may accept them and direct the secretary to make the necessary changes.

4. If the Chair desires the minutes to be verified by resolution, he asks for a motion to verify. Only persons who were present at the meeting may properly move, second, or vote on the motion.

5. The minutes of the meeting will record the verification of the minutes of the previous meeting.

   Chair:

   "You have received [*or* heard] the minutes (of the previous meeting). Are there any errors or omissions? If there are no objections I will verify them as correct"; *or*

   "The minutes stand verified as read."

   (*If the Chair desires a motion*):

   "You have heard the minutes. Are there any errors or omissions? Will someone move that the minutes of meeting held on [*date*] be verified as correct?"

(ii) *Motion to verify*

"I move that the minutes of the meeting of members held on [*date*] be hereby verified."

146

(iii) *Motion to verify with amendments*

"I move that the motion to verify be amended by adding the words . . .," *or*

"I move that the motion to verify be amended by deleting the words . . .," *or*

"I move that the motion to verify be amended by deleting the words . . . and substituting the words . . . ."

Rule 27.6 Alterations to Minutes

If it is discovered later that the minutes are incorrect, even after they have been verified, they may be altered, but only with the approval of a meeting, preferably the next meeting. Only those who were present at the meeting in question may move, second, or vote on the motion to alter the minutes. Minutes should never be altered otherwise, or have pages removed or added, without the prior approval of a meeting. *To expunge from the minutes in order to avoid possible embarrassment, see Rule 25.5, Expunging from Minutes, page 137.*

CHAPTER 28

Ejection from Meetings

¶ 2800 Introduction

Every meeting has the right to determine who may attend, under the provisions of the constitution. Members have a basic right to attend, invitees have a temporary conditional right, strangers and trespassers have no right.

Rule 28.1 Right to Eject

It is the duty of the Chair to preserve order (*Rule 10.2, Duties of Chair, page 44*). To do so, the Chair has the right to eject from the meeting

- members who become unruly (*Rule 28.2*);

- persons who have been invited but whose invitations have been revoked (*Rule 28.3*);

- strangers and trespassers (*Rule 28.4*).

Once the Chair has ordered a person to leave the meeting place, that person becomes a trespasser. The Chair should first warn him, and if he does not leave, he should then direct some other person or persons to eject the unwanted person and prevent him from re-entering.

In removing an unwanted person from the meeting place, only such reasonable force as is necessary may be used.

The Chair may, but is not obligated to, ask for the concurrence of the meeting to his order to eject the unwanted person.

149

Rule 28.2 Ejecting a Member

If a member unduly interferes with the reasonable conduct of a meeting, or prevents the orderly transaction of business, the Chair may have him ejected (*see Rule 28.1*) from the meeting and kept from re-entering the meeting place.

Rule 28.3 Ejecting an Invitee

If a person who has been invited to the meeting becomes unruly, interfering with the reasonable conduct of the meeting, or preventing the orderly transaction of business, the Chair may revoke the invitation and order him to leave the meeting room.

If the unruly invitee refuses to leave the meeting room after being warned, he may be ejected (*see Rule 28.1*).

Rule 28.4 Ejecting a Stranger

A stranger has no right to be present at society meetings. When he is requested by the Chair to leave, he must do so immediately.

Whether or not a stranger is conducting himself in an orderly fashion, he is a trespasser and ought to be ejected (*see Rule 28.1*).

For expulsion from the society, see Rule 5.4, Expulsion, page 17.

PART III

STRATEGY

CHAPTER 29

Strategic Manoeuvres

¶ 2900   Introduction

This chapter sets out manoeuvres which a member may use to accomplish various objectives in the conduct of the Society's business and affairs.

¶ 2905   Lobbying

No matter how worthy or important your proposal is, it is ineffective if other members of the same mind do not attend the meeting and vote for your proposal. Support for any proposal must be arranged in advance. Convincing uninformed or unconcerned voters is not an easy chore. You must educate members about the merits of your proposal, and convince them of the importance of attending the meeting and voting in favour of your proposal, or convince them to give you their proxies.

¶ 2910   Getting Your Motion on the Agenda

If a member desires to introduce new business which does not require special notice to the members, he may bring a motion that the subject of the new business be added to the agenda (*Rule 13.5, Adding to the Agenda, page 67*).

Instead of bringing a formal motion, a member may simply request the Chair to add the new item to the agenda, provided that no one objects, and provided that it is not an item that requires special notice. However, if the Chair is of the opinion that the proposed item is neither minor nor routine, then *all* members (present *and* absent) must waive notice before the item can be added to the agenda.

If the subject-matter of your proposed motion is already on the agenda, you may propose a motion on the subject as soon as the item is announced by the Chair.

¶ 2915   Strategic Uses of Motions

The following table sets out the motion which may be used to accomplish various objectives in the conduct of a meeting:

Objective	*Motion*	*Rule*
Introduce business	Main motion	17.4

All new business starts with a main motion (*Rule 17.2, Main Motions, page 85*). A member who wants the society to do something, to order something to be done, or to express an opinion about something, makes his wish known by means of a motion. A main motion originates business, directs or authorizes something to be done, adopts, ratifies, approves, and confirms or rejects reports, minutes, acts or things done.

Objective	*Motion*	*Rule*
Change a pending motion	Amend motion	18.1
	Divide motion	17.9
	Withdraw motion	17.10

Motions can be amended before being voted on, but the changes must be relevant to the motion (*see Chapter 18, Amendments, page 91*). After the motion has been discussed at the meeting, it may become apparent that the wording is not wholly acceptable to the meeting, or that it does not fully represent the wishes of the meeting. To remedy these situations, the motion may be amended.

Sometimes a motion may be amended in a such a manner as to effectively defeat the motion on the floor by making the entire motion wholly unacceptable to the meeting. This is often referred to as a "crippling amendment". However, a motion to amend cannot merely negate the original motion (*Rule 18.2, Conditions of Amendments, page 93*).

Sometimes a motion contains parts that are acceptable and parts that are not acceptable to a majority of the members. The proponents of one clause may find it advisable to have the motion divided into two or more parts and have each part voted on separately. If this is done, the most acceptable part will not be dragged down by the less acceptable part (*see Rule 17.9, Dividing a Motion, page 88*). The consent of the original mover or seconder of the motion is not necessary for the purpose of dividing the motion.

Objective	*Motion*	*Rule*
Delay or stop discussion on a motion	Withdraw motion	17.10
	Demands	15.2, 21.2-21.7
	Object to consideration	20.1
	Table a motion	20.2
	Postpone discussion	20.3
	Postpone discussion indefinitely	20.4
	Limit discussion	20.5
	Vote immediately	20.6
	Refer or refer back	20.7
	Closing motions	26.1–26.7

If discussion becomes too protracted, heated, or embarrassing, or if it is going the wrong way, there are rules which can create a breather, apart from recessing or adjourning. Discussion may be cut off abruptly (with or without a vote being taken on the original motion), postponed to a fixed time, or limited or suspended temporarily.

Objective	*Demand*	*Rule*
Prevent irregularity in procedure	Point of order	21.6
Object to insulting or abusive comments	Point of personal privilege	21.2
Object to any matter affecting the member's comfort or convenience	Point of general privilege	21.3
Ask for information	Point of information	21.4
Ask for correct procedure to be followed	Point of procedure (Parliamentary inquiry)	21.5
Correct an error made by the Chair or a previous speaker	Correct an error	21.7
Question the presence of a quorum	Quorum count	15.2

Demands attract the immediate attention of the Chair. Discussion is suspended until the Chair determines their validity and deals with them. The following are the more common demands:

Objective	**Motion**	**Rule**
Suppress a motion	Withdraw motion	17.10
	Object to consideration	20.1
	Postpone discussion indefinitely	20.4

It is sometimes possible to suppress a motion without bringing it to a vote. For example, before it has been stated by the Chair, a motion (or an amendment) may be withdrawn or amended by the mover. After it has been stated by the Chair, a motion may be withdrawn or amended by the mover only if no one objects. If anyone objects, a formal motion must be made to withdraw or amend the main motion.

A member who feels that a motion is inopportune, embarrassing, or unnecessary may object (by motion) to consideration of the main motion.

The following motions may also be used to suppress other motions:

● rule motion out of order (*Rule 17.1, page 84*)

● postpone discussion (*Rule 20.3, page 103*)

● postpone discussion indefinitely (*Rule 20.4, page 103*)

● refer or refer back (*Rule 20.7, page 106*)

● close meeting (*Rules 26.1–26.4, pages 139 to 141*)

● amend by attaching a crippling amendment (*see "Change a pending motion", page 154*)

Objective	**Motion**	**Rule**
Enforce rights	Point of personal privilege	21.2
	Point of general privilege	21.3
	Point of information	21.4
	Point of procedure	21.5
	Point of order	21.6

(*See "Delay or stop discussion on a motion", page 155.*)

Objective	*Motion*	*Rule*
Review actions	Reconsider resolution	25.2
	Rescind resolution	25.3
	Reconsider defeated motion	25.1

Sometimes the members, having passed a resolution or defeated a motion at the same or a previous meeting, wish to reconsider the question for any one of a number of reasons: the matter was dealt with too hastily, the meeting was not truly representative of the members, or conditions have changed. Only main motions (*Rule 17.2, Main Motions, page 85*) can be reviewed.

A resolution cannot be reviewed, however, if it authorized a payment to be made and the payment has been made, or if it elected or appointed someone to an office and that person was present at the meeting or has been notified of his election or appointment, or if the resolution approved a contract and the other party to the contract was present at the meeting or has been notified of the result of the resolution respecting the contract.

If the proposal to review the resolution or motion takes place at a subsequent meeting, and the resolution or motion that is sought to be reviewed required notice to be given to the members, notice of the proposal to review must be given in the same manner as the notice required for the original motion.

Objective	*Motion*	*Rule*
Close the meeting	Conclude meeting	26.4
	Adjourn to an unfixed date (*sine die*)	26.3
	Adjourn to a fixed date	26.2

A motion to conclude the meeting dissolves the meeting permanently. A motion to adjourn suspends the meeting until it is reconvened on the day fixed by the motion. A motion to recess suspends the meeting for a short period only, as in the case of a lunch break, waiting for ballots to be counted, permitting private negotiations to be carried on, allowing members to "cool off", etc.

157

¶ 2920　Requisitioned Meetings, Motions, and Circulated Statements

In many societies, the governing statute, the constitution, or the bylaws give the members a right to convene a meeting of members, upon obtaining the signatures of a small percentage of the members on a "requisition" (petition). Such requisitioned meetings are becoming more common as members of societies become increasingly aware of their rights. Frequently, the purpose of a requisitioned meeting is to remove the board of directors when the board has lost the confidence and support of the membership. (*See Rule 6.9(iii), Removal of Directors, Requisitioned Meeting, page 22, and Rule 7.8(v), Requisitioned Meeting to Remove Officers, page 30.*)

In many societies, members also have the right to require the board of directors

(a) to give notice, to all members, of any motion that may properly be moved and is intended to be moved at the next scheduled meeting of members; and,

(b) to circulate, to all members, a statement commenting on any proposed motion or any business to be dealt with at the next scheduled meeting of members.

The statute, constitution, or bylaw authorizing the requisitioned meeting, motion, or circulated statement, must be strictly complied with.

CHAPTER 30

How to Conduct a Meeting of Members

¶ 3000 Introduction

This chapter outlines the basic elements of conducting an amicable, routine, and non-contentious meeting of a society (or a club or association).

For the sake of simplicity, let us assume that the society has adopted a code of rules of order (*see ¶ 320, Adoption of Rules of Order, page 12*) that a proper notice of meeting has been sent (*see Chapter 12, Notice of General Meetings, page 59*), and that an agenda was either sent with the notice or distributed before the meeting (*see Chapter 13, Agendas, page 65*).

¶ 3005 Calling the Meeting to Order

The meeting is called to order by the person designated by the bylaws/constitution (usually the President or Chair). If no Chair has been designated, or if the designated Chair and his substitute (usually the Vice-President) are not present, *see Rule 10.1, Chair at Meetings, page 44.* The Chair stands at the rostrum or table, and says:

"The meeting will please come to order. This is the regular monthly meeting of the .... Society. In accordance with the constitution, I, as President, will act as the Chair [*or*, in the absence of the President and the Vice-President, we will proceed to appoint a substitute Chair]." (*See Chapter 10, The Chair, page 43*).

159

¶ 3010 Appointment of Secretary

The Chair appoints a secretary of the meeting (usually the secretary of the society).

"Mr./Ms. A will act as secretary of the meeting."

¶ 3015 Checking the Quorum

The Chair, with the help of the secretary and/or the scrutineers, verifies that there is a quorum present in accordance with the bylaws (*see Chapter 15, Quorum, page 73*).

"According to the bylaws, a quorum is [*number*]. There is a quorum present [*or*, I am advised that there is a quorum present]. Since the meeting is duly constituted, we will now proceed with the meeting."

If a quorum is not present, the meeting should be adjourned or converted into an information meeting (*Rule 15.1, Quorum Present, page 73*).

¶ 3020 Approving the Agenda

The Chair asks the meeting to consider and approve the agenda (which was distributed before the meeting). *See Chapter 13, Agendas, page 65.*

"Each of you has received a copy of the Agenda. Would anyone like to add anything? Would anyone like to change the order for discussion?"

Items in the agenda may be renumbered (to change the order) by a resolution of the meeting. Items that do require special notice under the constitution cannot be added or deleted without the consent of all members, present and absent (*see Rule 13.4, Renumbering the Agenda, page 66*).

¶ 3025 Verification of Minutes

If required by the bylaws (it is not required by any law), the minutes of the previous meeting may be submitted for correction of errors or addition of items omitted, and for approval.

"The secretary will read the minutes of the last meeting held on [*date*] [*or*, The minutes of the last meeting held on [*date*] have been distributed to the members]. You have read (or heard) the minutes. Are there any corrections or additions?"

(After discussion is finished and all changes have been made):

"The Chair will entertain a motion that the minutes of the meeting held on [*date*] be verified."

¶ 3030 Reports from Committees

"The next item on the agenda is consideration of committee reports. We will now consider the report of the [*name*] committee. The Chair of the committee will please give his report."

After the report has been read or distributed, the Chair will ask

"Are there any questions you would like to put to the Chair of the [*name*] committee?"

When all questions have been answered, the Chair asks

"May I have a motion to adopt the report of the [*name*] committee? [*add if desired:* and to direct or authorize the board to (*set out action desired*).]"

Repeat for the report of every committee.

¶ 3035 Correspondence

"Has the (Corresponding) Secretary anything to report on correspondence?"

(After his report is concluded):

"Do you have any questions? How would the meeting like to deal with the matter?"

"A motion is in order to authorize [*or* instruct] the Secretary to [*set out action desired*]."

¶ 3040 Business Arising Out of Minutes

The Chair should review any items of business in the minutes of the previous meeting (apart from committee reports) that require further consideration or follow-up, and may ask the person responsible for the item if he has anything to report.

¶ 3045   New Matters

See Rule 13.4, Renumbering the Agenda, page 66. The Chair does not have any duty to ask for items of new business, unless the governing statute specifically gives members the right to raise any item of business at a meeting. If so, the Chair should ask

"Is there any new business anyone would like to bring up?"

Repeat procedure as necessary.

¶ 3050   Conclusion

"Is there any further business to discuss?"

When the Chair is of the opinion that there is no other business to be brought up, he declares

"If there is no further business, the meeting is now concluded" *or,*

"A motion to conclude the meeting is now in order" (*see Chapter 26, Closing the Meeting, page 139*).

A motion to conclude the meeting is not necessary if all business on the agenda has been dealt with.

PART IV

SPECIAL SOCIETIES

CHAPTER 31

Condominium Corporations*

A. Formation and Organization

¶3100 Introduction

All provinces in Canada have legislation dealing with condominium-style co-ownership of land. Condominiums are a unique form of co-ownership in that each co-owner has the exclusive ownership of, as well as the exclusive right to occupy, a specific portion of the condominium

---

* This chapter was written in consultation with Jonathan H. Fine, B.Sc., LL.B.

property. Unfortunately, not all provinces use the same terminology; even the term "condominium" is not used in all provinces (for example, in **Quebec**, the condominium concept is described as "co-ownership of immoveables established by declaration"). In this chapter, the terminology used in the **Ontario** *Condominium Act* will be used in enunciating general principles of condominium law and procedure. Examples of differing terminology from other provinces will be given, but such examples are not intended to be exhaustive.

There are substantial similarities, but also substantial differences, among the various provincial condominium statutes in Canada. Every director, member, officer and employee of a condominium would be well advised to purchase a copy of the applicable provincial condominium statute (from the provincial government bookstore or Queen's Printer). A careful reading of the statute and this chapter will give any condominium director, member, officer or employee a good general understanding of what goes on at condominium meetings and what he or she can do if he or she does not like the way the condominium, or the condominium meetings, are being run.

The provincial condominium statutes reviewed in this chapter are:

Alta: *Condominium Property Act*, R.S.A. 1980, c. C-22

B.C.: *Condominium Act*, R.S.B.C. 1979, c. 61

Man.: *Condominium Act*, R.S.M. 1987, c. C170

N.B.: *Condominium Property Act*, R.S.N.B. 1973, c. C-16

N.S.: *Condominium Act*, R.S.N.S. 1989, c. 85

Ont.: *Condominium Act*, R.S.O. 1990, c. C.26

Que.: *Civil Code*, Chap. III, "of Co-ownership of Immoveables Established by Declaration"

Sask.: *Condominium Property Act*, R.S.S. 1978, c. C-26

The condominium concept (which may be applied to residences as well as to commercial, industrial and resort projects) is a means by which the property is divided into units, which are individually owned, and common elements, which are owned by all the unit owners as tenants in common who share expenses according to their respective interests in the condominium.

¶ 3105 Definitions

"**Common elements**" means the parts of the property which are owned by all the unit owners as tenants in common and are available for the use of all the owners. They can include the foundation, roof, heating and air-conditioning equipment, elevators, corridors, access areas, gardens, driveways, parking spaces, and any other property not defined in the declaration as being a "unit" for individual ownership.

The **British Columbia, Alberta** and **Saskatchewan** statutes refer to this as "common property". **B.C.** and **Saskatchewan** legislation use the term "common facility" to describe a facility available for the use of all the owners (for example, a swimming pool). **Manitoba** and **Ontario** use the term "common elements", while **Quebec** uses the term "common portions".

"**Common expenses**" means all expenses arising from the duties and objects of the condominium corporation, and expenses which are deemed common expenses by the condominium statute or the declaration.

The term "common expenses" is used in **B.C., Alberta, Manitoba, Ontario, Nova Scotia** and **New Brunswick**. In **Saskatchewan**, the legislation refers to "administrative expenses".

"**Common interest**" means each unit owner's proportionate interest in the common elements as set out in the declaration.

In **B.C.**, the term is "unit settlement". **Alberta** and **Saskatchewan** use the term "unit factor".

"**Condominium**" consists of

(a) individual units (housing, commercial or industrial), individually owned by members of the condominium corporation, and

(b) common elements owned by all of the unit owners collectively as "tenants in common".

"**Declaration**" is the incorporating document of a condominium corporation, equivalent to articles of incorporation, letters patent or memorandum of association of a business corporation.

Manitoba, Ontario, Nova Scotia and **New Brunswick** all have legislation that requires a declaration. The **Quebec** *Civil Code* requires a declaration, but this declaration does not create a corporation; it establishes the scheme of co-ownership of the immoveable property without using a corporate structure. In **B.C.**, the deposit of the "strata plan", and in **Alberta** and **Saskatchewan**, the registration of the "condominium plan" in the appropriate land titles office creates the corporation. In

B.C., Alberta and **Saskatchewan**, the mandatory initial bylaws cover most of the matters that are dealt with in the declaration in **Manitoba, Ontario, Nova Scotia** and **New Brunswick**.

"**Description**" consists of a survey of the land and buildings which comprise the condominium, and a set of as-built architectural plans.

In **B.C.**, this is referred to as the "strata plan", and in **Alberta** and **Saskatchewan**, it is referred to as the "condominium plan". In **Manitoba**, it is referred to simply as the "plan".

"**Rules**" are a set of positive and negative obligations relating to the use of the common elements and units, to promote the safety, security, and welfare of the unit owners and of the property, and to prevent unreasonable interference with the use and enjoyment of the common elements and of the units.

¶ 3110   Creation of Condominium Corporations

In most provinces, a condominium corporation is created by the registration of a declaration and a description. In **Quebec**, there are no "condominium corporations"; the registration of a declaration (in **Quebec**) establishes the scheme of co-ownership of the property, without using a corporate structure.

¶ 3115   Personal Liability

Unlike business corporations whose shareholders are not responsible for the liabilities of the business corporation, the unit owners (members) of a condominium corporation are responsible for the liabilities of the condominium corporation in the percentages set out in the declaration (or plan, as the case may be).

For example, if a judgment for the payment of money is obtained against a condominium corporation, a proportion of the judgment is enforceable against each unit owner at the time that the cause of action arose (in **Manitoba** and **Quebec**), at the time of the judgment (in **Ontario**), or at the time of execution of the judgment (in **British Columbia, Alberta** and **Saskatchewan**). The proportion enforceable against each unit owner is the same proportion specified in the declaration (or plan) for sharing the common interests and expenses.

168

¶ 3120   Bylaws and Rules

(a) Bylaws

The board may pass bylaws which are reasonable and consistent with the condominium statute and the declaration.

In **British Columbia**, the statute prescribes mandatory initial bylaws of the strata corporation. These mandatory initial bylaws may be amended or repealed, but only in the manner set out in the statute and the bylaws, and only by the required majority (either 75 percent or 100 percent). In **Alberta**, the statute also prescribes mandatory initial bylaws, which may be amended, repealed or replaced by a special resolution. In **Saskatchewan**, the statute establishes mandatory initial bylaws, but these may be amended only by unanimous resolution. In **Manitoba**, bylaws can be made or amended by a vote of members who own a minimum of 66⅔ percent of the units. In **Ontario**, bylaws require confirmation "by owners who own not less than fifty-one percent of the units at a meeting duly called for that purpose". This provision would appear to require that fifty-one percent of *all* the unit owners (not merely those in attendance at the meeting) must vote in favour of confirmation of the bylaw.

However, a recent **Ontario** District Court decision, in interpreting a similarly-worded provision dealing with removal of directors, held that if a majority of unit owners attend the meeting, and if a majority of those in attendance at the meeting vote in favour of the motion, then the motion for removal is carried. Since this issue has not been adjudicated upon by a higher court, this decision should not be relied on as conclusive. In **Quebec**, there are no "condominium corporations" and therefore no bylaws as such. In **Nova Scotia** and **New Brunswick**, bylaws can also be made or amended by a vote of members who own at least 66⅔ percent of the units.

Where any provision in a bylaw is inconsistent with the condominium statute or the declaration, the statute or the declaration prevails, and the bylaw (or the offending portion of the bylaw) is deemed to be of no effect. For example, bylaws cannot provide for any contribution to common expenses not in the proportions specified in the declaration. Bylaws also cannot provide for any higher or lower majorities for the passing of motions at meetings of unit owners than is specified in the condominium statute. However, the statute may permit a higher majority to be specified in the declaration.

(b) Rules

See definition "Rules", above.

In all provinces, except **Ontario**, the "rules" are part of the declaration (however described) or the bylaws.

The **Ontario** *Condominium Act* provides that the board make rules ("house rules") affecting the use of the common elements. The rules must be:

- reasonable and consistent with the condominium statute, the declaration, and the bylaws;

- designed to promote the safety, security, or welfare of the owners and of the property, or to prevent unreasonable interference with the use and enjoyment of the common elements and of the other units;

- neither arbitrary nor discriminatory.

The rules must be complied with, and may be enforced, in the same manner as the bylaws, for example, by an application pursuant to section 49 of the **Ontario** *Condominium Act*.

¶3125   Board of Directors

The business and affairs of the condominium corporation are managed by a committee which may be designated a board of directors, or by some other name. In **Ontario**, it is called a board of directors. In **British Columbia**, the term "strata council" is used. In **Alberta** and **Saskatchewan**, the board is described as the "board of managers". The term "administrators" is used in **Quebec**, but these administrators are not corporate directors since there are no condominium corporations in **Quebec**.

Directors are elected at meetings of unit owners (usually at the annual meeting). The procedure for election of directors of condominium boards is similar to that of other societies (*see Chapter 6, Directors, page 19*). Directors need not be unit owners unless the constitution requires them to be.

In **British Columbia**, only unit owners are eligible to be on the strata council. In **Alberta**, non-owners are eligible as long as two of the seven board members are owners. In **Saskatchewan**, the board consists of not less than three and not more than seven owners. In **Manitoba**, **Ontario**, **Nova Scotia** and **New Brunswick**, the legislation does not require that directors be unit owners. The **Quebec** *Civil Code* does not require administrators to be co-proprietors (unit owners).

¶ 3130   Officers

The officers of the condominium corporation are elected or appointed by the board of directors, however designated.

In **British Columbia**, the mandatory initial bylaws require the strata council to elect a chairman and a vice-chairman from among the members of the strata council. In **Alberta**, the mandatory initial bylaws provide that the members of the board must designate from among themselves a president, vice-president, secretary and treasurer. In **Saskatchewan**, neither the statute nor the mandatory initial bylaws require that any officers be elected or appointed, except that, under the initial mandatory bylaws, the board at the commencement of each board meeting must elect a chairman for the meeting, and at the commencement of each general meeting must elect a chairman of the meeting. In **Manitoba, Nova Scotia** and **New Brunswick**, there are no mandatory officers, but the declaration may require or authorize specific officers to be elected or appointed. In **Ontario**, the corporation must have a president (who must be a director, unless the bylaws provide otherwise) and a secretary. Other officers may be required or authorized by bylaw or by resolution of the board. The **Quebec** *Civil Code* is silent regarding officers.

¶ 3135   Manager

The board of directors may delegate its management duties to a unit owner, an employee, or a professional property manager or management corporation.

¶ 3140   Committees

A committee is a body (of one or more members) to which the appointing body delegates one or more of its functions. (*See also Chapter 8, Committees, page 31.*) Most condominium corporations find it useful to have several committees, in order to assist the board and to involve more of the unit owners in the management of their condominium project.

"Standing committees" are committees which continue in operation for as long as the condominium corporation is in existence, unless the constitution provides otherwise.

"Special committees" (or "*ad hoc* committees") are appointed for a specific task and remain in existence only until the task is concluded and they report to the body which appointed them. The members of a standing committee or a special committee may be appointed, removed, or replaced at the will of the appointing body.

The following are examples of standing committees in a condominium corporation and their functions:

(i) Finance Committee

The functions of the finance committee are to monitor the financial affairs of the corporation; to review the financial statements; to work closely with the corporation's auditors; and to set up budgets and to advise the board thereon. This committee (sometimes called the Budget Review Committee) should include the treasurer and persons with some accounting or business experience.

(ii) Building Committee

The functions of the Building Committee are to receive complaints concerning defects in the construction of the units and common elements; to supervise architects and engineers retained by the corporation; and to investigate warranties given in respect of the workmanship and materials used in construction of the property.

This committee is very important during the first years of the building. Its investigations provide the best evidence in any dispute with the developer or builder.

(iii) Legal Committee

The functions of the Legal Committee are to investigate and advise on contracts to be signed by the corporation; to act as liaison to the corporation's solicitor; to deal with breaches of the statute, declaration, and rules; and to investigate the facts in lawsuits brought against the corporation or intended to be brought by the corporation.

This committee should consist of lawyers and persons with business experience.

(iv) Rules Committee

The functions of the Rules Committee are to prepare and revise house rules for submission to the board; and to receive and investigate infractions of the rules, and to negotiate with the persons responsible in order to have them corrected.

This committee should consist of homemakers who have lived in apartment buildings and condominiums, lawyers, and people with writing skills.

(v) Maintenance Committee

The functions of the Maintenance Committee are to oversee the housekeeping, appearance, and cleanliness of the buildings, lobbies, halls, and other common elements; and to oversee the care given to the house plants and the garden plants.

This committee (sometimes called the Housekeeping Committee) checks the work of the cleaning staff and the gardeners. A representative from each floor or group of buildings would add to the efficiency of this committee.

Homemakers and persons with green thumbs are best suited for this committee.

(vi) Social Committee

The functions of the Social Committee are to welcome new occupants to the condominium and to familiarize them with its facilities and rules; and to arrange social affairs, bridge parties, exercise classes, and other get-togethers.

This committee encourages occupants to participate in condominium activities.

(vii) Community Committee

The functions of the Community Committee are to disseminate information and notices from the board to the occupants; to supervise the calling of annual and special meetings; and to supervise the publication of a newsletter.

This committee (also called the Information Committee, Newsletter Committee, and/or Publication Committee) should, if possible, include the secretary and persons who have some experience in running an office, as well as writers.

As the corporation is responsible for the content of the newsletter (libel, misstatements, fraudulent or misleading advertisements, etc.), this committee must carefully supervise everything that goes into print. Nothing should be published unless approved by the vote of a majority of the committee at a meeting called for that purpose. Above all, no one editor ought to be given free rein.

B. Meetings of Unit Owners

¶ 3145   Voting and Voting Principles

(a) Method of Voting

In most provinces, votes at meetings of unit owners are taken by a show of hands, unless a poll is demanded by at least one unit owner or proxyholder. Unless the constitution provides otherwise, votes on a show of hands are on the basis of one vote per unit. However, a demand for a poll supersedes a vote by a show of hands, even if the vote has already been completed.

(b) Number of Votes Per Unit

In **Ontario**, voting by unit owners is on the basis of one vote per unit, regardless of the unit owner's proportionate common interest; the owner of a large unit and the owner of a small unit each have one vote.

In **Alberta**, the number of votes that a unit owner may cast on a poll shall correspond to the unit factors for the respective units represented by that person. In other words, owners of larger units have more votes than owners of smaller units. **Saskatchewan** and **Quebec** use the same approach as **Alberta**. This is a deviation from the "one member one vote" principle applicable to most societies.

The **Manitoba** and **Nova Scotia** statutes leave it to the declarant to specify (in the declaration) whether "one vote per unit" or "percentage common interest" voting will be used at meetings of unit owners.

The **British Columbia** and **New Brunswick** statutes are silent about this; therefore, this matter may be dealt with in the bylaws in those provinces.

(c) Co-Owners

Where two or more persons entitled to vote in respect of one unit disagree on their vote, the vote in respect of that unit shall not be counted.

(d) Owners in Arrears

Some condominium statutes (e.g., **Ontario** *Condominium Act*, subsection 22(5)) provide that a unit owner who is in default of payment of common expenses is not entitled to vote, except on matters requiring a unanimous vote of all unit owners.

(e) Voting Majorities

Generally, all questions proposed for consideration of the owners at a meeting of unit owners shall be determined by a majority of the votes cast, unless the constitution provides that some other plurality or percentage is required. The bylaws cannot require a higher percentage of votes on any matter than is required by the statute. However, the statute may permit a higher majority to be specified in the declaration.

The chair of the meeting should be familiar with the statute in order to determine what majority is required on any particular motion.

¶ 3150   Quorum

The following are quorum requirements for meetings of unit owners in several Canadian provinces:

British Columbia: ⅓ of unit owners

Alberta: ¼ of unit owners

Saskatchewan: ½ of unit owners

Ontario: ⅓ of unit owners

Quorum requirements for the other provinces are outlined in the declaration or bylaws.

¶ 3155   Notice of Meetings

Most condominium statutes (e.g., **B.C.**, **Alberta**, **Saskatchewan**, **Ontario** and **Quebec**) provide that a minimum period of ten days' written notice of every meeting of unit owners be given to each owner and to each mortgagee entitled to vote. These statutes also specify what the notice is required to contain (for example, the place, date, time and purpose of the meeting). The **Ontario** *Condominium Act* and the **Quebec** *Civil Code* specify the method of service of the notice of meeting. In most other provinces, the method of service is dealt with in the declaration or bylaws.

Meetings of unit owners may be called by the board. In some jurisdictions, the statute provides that meetings of unit owners may also be called by the mortgagees of such percentage of the units as is specified in the statute (in **British Columbia**, 25 percent; in **Ontario**, 15 percent). The declaration or bylaws may contain a similar provision even in those provinces where the statute does not specifically confer this right upon mortgagees.

The declaration or bylaws may provide for regularly-scheduled meetings on a monthly, quarterly or some other periodic basis. (*For requisitioned meetings, see ¶ 3185 below.*)

¶ 3160   Annual Meetings

Most of the condominium statutes provide that the first annual meeting of owners must be held within a specific period of time after the registration of the declaration (in **Ontario**, three months), and subsequent annual meetings must be held at a specified period of time after the previous annual general meeting (in **Ontario**, fifteen months).

The order of business for meetings of unit owners is sometimes set out in the bylaws. For a sample agenda, see Appendix B, Form CO–8, page 239. See also Chapter 16, Meetings of Members, page 77.

Some of the provincial condominium statutes provide that any owner or mortgagee entitled to vote may raise any matter relevant to the affairs and business of the corporation at any annual meeting (*see Rule 13.5, Adding to the Agenda, page 67*).

The following is a recommended procedure for the calling of an annual meeting in **Ontario**. A similar procedure may be adopted for other provinces.

1. The provisions of the provincial condominium statute must be strictly observed.

2. At least ten days' written notice must be given to each unit owner and mortgagee who is entitled to vote under the terms of the mortgage. The notice must specify the nature of the business to be presented at the meeting and must be given personally or by prepaid mail. In the case of joint owners, a separate envelope (containing all the necessary material) must be sent to each owner. If the condominium record is incomplete or not up-to-date, the names and addresses of the unit owners and mortgagees may be verified at the local Land Registry Office.

3. For meetings where there will be one or more complicated issues dealt with, an *information circular* should be sent to the unit owners and mortgagees, together with the usual *agenda, proxyform, and notice of meeting*. Unit owners should be canvassed before the meeting to ascertain whether they will be attending, and if not, whether they will be delivering proxies. The canvassing of unit owners is important to ensure that there will be a quorum for the meeting, and particularly for any motion requiring that a specified percentage (higher than the ordinary quorum) of unit owners be present at the meeting.

4. The condominium corporation must send a copy of the *latest financial statement and auditor's report* to the unit owners at least ten days before the date of the annual general meeting. The statement must comply in every respect with the bylaws. Many condominium corporations send this information with the notice of meeting, proxyform, information circular, and agenda.

¶ 3165 Special Meetings

A "special meeting" of unit owners is a meeting called to consider a specific important item of business. The business of a special meeting, apart from the opening and closing formalities, may consist solely of the item which the meeting was called to consider. (*See Appendix A, Forms S–14 and S–15, page 220.*)

¶ 3170 Regular Meetings

The declaration or bylaws may provide for regularly scheduled meetings of unit owners on a monthly, quarterly, or some other periodic basis. However, it is not appropriate to give a single notice for two or more regularly scheduled future meetings, since the unit owners or mortgagees entitled to vote may change between meetings.

¶ 3175 Proxies

Most constitutions provide that unit owners may vote either in person or by proxy at meetings of unit owners.

A proxy is a written authorization to the holder of the proxy to vote in place of the person entitled to vote at the meeting. Most constitutions do not prescribe a form of proxy. Forms CO–4 (page 241) and CO–5 (page 242) are suggested proxyforms.

Proxies may be either:

(a) limited, so that the proxyholder may vote only on specific questions and/or may vote only a certain way; and

(b) unlimited, so that the proxyholder may vote on any question and in any way the proxyholder sees fit.

It is usual for a form of proxy to accompany the note of meeting; however, proxies need not be in the form sent with the notice of meeting.

Where important issues are to be voted on at the meeting, it is recommended that a concerted effort be made prior to the meeting to obtain sufficient proxies to ensure a majority vote in favour of the position that you are advocating.

See also Chapter 14, Proxies, page 69.

¶ 3180   Nominations for Directors

1. After determining how many positions will be open for election to the board of directors, the board of directors *may*, but need not, request that nominations of potential candidates be deposited in writing with the secretary (or the manager) prior to the meeting.

2. In any event, whether advance nominations are made, nominations for the position of director will be made at the meeting.

3. A person need not be at the meeting where he or she is elected to the board of directors to be validly elected.

4. In order to be validly elected to the board of directors:

    (a) if present at the meeting, he or she must not have refused to act as a director; or

    (b) if not present at the meeting, he or she must have consented to act either before the election or within ten days thereafter.

¶ 3185   Requisitioned Meetings

The condominium statutes in most provinces permit a specified percentage of unit owners to requisition a meeting of unit owners. The board is required to call and hold such a meeting within a specified period, failing which any of the requisitionists may call the meeting to be held within a specified period after the receipt of the requisition by the board.

In **British Columbia,** 25 percent of the unit owners may requisition a meeting; in **Alberta,** 15 percent; in **Saskatchewan,** 25 percent; in **Ontario,** 15 percent.

In **Ontario,** if the board fails to call the requisitioned meeting, any of the requisitionists may call the meeting; in other jurisdictions, a court application may be required.

The **Quebec** *Civil Code* provides that if the declaration does not provide otherwise, a special meeting may be called by those co-proprietors (unit owners) holding one-quarter of the votes.

In those provinces in which the statute does not provide for requisitioned meetings, the declaration or bylaws may contain such a provision.

In those provinces in which the statute does provide for requisitioned meetings but does not provide that the requisitionists may call a meeting if the board refuses, the bylaws may contain such a provision.

Any unit owners who wish to requisition such a meeting should consult the statute, the declaration and the bylaws for procedural requirements (time limits, contents of notice or requisition, method of service, etc.).

¶ 3190   Informational Sessions (Budget)

Each year, the board of directors must determine the anticipated expenses to be incurred by the condominium corporation in the forthcoming year, and determine what revenues will be required to cover those expenses and provide adequate reserves. The board then prepares and approves a formal budget. The consent of the unit owners to the budget is not necessary. However, it is prudent to call and hold an informational session concerning the budget and to circulate the budget with complete explanatory notes well in advance of the meeting. The more explanation that is given in the explanatory notes prior to the meeting, the more smoothly the informational session will proceed.

These informational sessions cannot be called "meetings" because no voting takes place.

C. Turnover by Declarant

¶ 3191   "Turnover Meeting"

The **Ontario** *Condominium Act* provides that as soon as the declarant ceases to be the registered owner of a majority of the units, the declarant must call a "turnover meeting" within 21 days, and that the meeting must be held within 21 days after it is called.

The **Ontario** statute is unique (in Canada) in specifically requiring the calling of a meeting, election of a new board, and the turnover of documents and the corporate seal as soon as the declarant (the person who filed the declaration that created the condominium) loses majority control. The **Nova Scotia** statute contains a turnover checklist similar to **Ontario's**, but does not require a turnover meeting or the election of a new board when the declarant loses majority control. At the turnover meeting, a new board is elected and the declarant must turn over to the new board the following items:

(i) the seal of the corporation;

(ii) the minute book for the corporation, containing the most up-to-date copies of the declaration, bylaws, rules and regulations;

(iii) copies of all agreements entered into by the corporation, the declarant, or his representatives on behalf of the corporation;

(iv) a record of the owners and their mailing addresses;

(v) the existing warranties and guarantees;

(vi) the as-built architectural, structural, engineering, mechanical, electrical and plumbing plans;

(vii) the original specifications indicating thereon all material changes;

(viii) the plans for underground site service, site grading, drainage and landscaping, together with cable television drawings, if available;

(ix) such other available plans and information relevant to future repair or maintenance of the property;

(x) an unaudited financial statement prepared as at a date not earlier than thirty days prior to the meeting;

(xi) a table depicting the maintenance responsibilities and indicating whether the corporation or the unit owners are responsible;

(xii) bills of sale or transfers for all items that are assets of the condominium corporation but not part of the real property;

(xiii) a list detailing current replacement costs and life expectancy under normal maintenance conditions of all major capital items in the property, including, where applicable, those items set out in subsection 1 of section 36; and

(xiv) all financial records of the corporation and of the declarant relating to the operation of the corporation from the date of registration of the declaration and the description.

Within 60 days after the meeting, the declarant must give to the new board an audited financial statement prepared as at the date of the meeting.

The new "turnover board" should meet as soon as possible afterwards and follow the procedure outlined in ¶ 3193.

¶ 3193　Procedure for Turnover Board

1. Receive all the items listed in ¶ 3191.

2. Study, to get a working knowledge of, the condominium statute, declaration, bylaws, management agreement, and insurance trust agreement. Study the declaration and bylaws for errors, inconsistencies, and possible improvements (e.g., "adults only", no pets, etc.). If necessary, enlist the help of a lawyer. Study (with the help of an insurance broker) the insurance trust agreement and all insurance policies. Ensure there is adequate coverage. Consider revising standard form insurance clauses to suit the condominium's needs. Consider indemnity insurance for directors and officers (and educational courses for directors and officers, in order to avoid liability claims).

3. Officers: Elect or appoint officers (see ¶ 3130).

4. Appoint a lawyer for the condominium corporation.

5. Manager: Review the management agreement. Consider appointing a new manager and negotiating a new management agreement. Review management procedures with manager.

6. Engineer: Retain an engineer to study the structural and engineering plans, and check utilities and maintenance. Investigate warranties on equipment. (Consult a lawyer if necessary.)

7. Prepare (or update) inventory of all equipment, furniture, appliances, and other chattels of the condominium corporation. Consider whether insurance coverage is adequate.

8. Ascertain whether the declarant retains any interest in the property (e.g., parking units, locker units, superintendent's suite). If so, ascertain what the declarant plans to do with his interest. Consider whether the condominium corporation should offer to purchase the declarant's remaining interest.

9. Records: Review all records of the condominium. Ensure that the list of owners and residents is up-to-date with all relevant information. Review board of directors' minute book and owners' minute book with lawyer, and make a note of the expiry of the terms of office of the directors.

10. Set policies: Procedures for meetings, frequency of board meetings, open or closed board meetings, preparation and signing of estoppel certificates. Set up proper collection procedures for common expenses. Establish a plan for the future (for the next year or few years). Adopt a set of rules of order to govern all

meetings of the board and of the unit owners (e.g., *Wainberg's Society Meetings including Rules of Order*).

11. Engage an auditor to review the financial records for the period prior to the turnover meeting. Review with the auditor the sufficiency of the existing reserve fund, the anticipated contributions to and expenditures from the reserve fund, and how the reserve fund is currently invested. Prepare a budget (with the assistance of the auditor and building manager).

12. Arrange for inspection by New Home Warranty Program (**Ontario**) or other government warranty authority.

13. Check tax assessments for individual units and common areas, and consider a joint appeal.

14. Order new letterheads and envelopes for the condominium corporation.

15. Send a report (or minutes) of the turnover meeting to all unit owners.

16. Call the first annual meeting of unit owners, following the procedure set out in ¶ 3160.

D. Finances

¶ 3195 Budget and Common Expenses

Shortly before the beginning of each financial year of the condominium corporation, the board of directors will prepare a budget of the estimated expenses of the condominium corporation for the coming year. Unit owners will then be notified of the estimated expenses for the upcoming year and of the amounts of their proportionate shares which they will be required to contribute monthly throughout the year.

¶ 3197 Special Assessments

Occasionally, expenses will arise that were not contemplated by the board of directors at the time that the board prepared the budget.

In these circumstances, the board of directors may decide to levy a "special assessment".

A special assessment is merely a requirement to pay an amount (usually in one lump sum or two or three instalments) over and above the regular monthly common expense amounts.

CHAPTER 32

Co-Operatives and Credit Unions*

A. Formation and Organization

¶3200 Definitions

- **"Co-operative"** is a democratically operated association of persons organized to furnish themselves (or themselves and others) with commodities or services.

- **"Credit unions"** are co-operative organizations that provide financial services to members and the public.

- **"Caisse populaires"** are co-operatives that operate in Quebec.

---

* This chapter was written by Garry Gillam, LL.B.

183

¶ 3205 Introduction

Traditionally, one thinks of three forms of business enterprise: sole proprietorships, partnerships, and corporations. There is, however, another form of business enterprise which has become important in the Canadian economy. Co-operative organizations are now involved in everything from yogurt to insurance services. In fact, in 1990, the Canadian co-operative system was estimated to have assets in excess of sixty-two billion dollars, the largest component of which is the credit union/caisse populaire system. However, the presence of co-operative enterprise in the Canadian economy very often goes unnoticed.

There are two facets of co-operative enterprises which make these enterprises unique in the business world. Firstly, irrespective of the number of shares that a shareholder may have, each shareholder is accorded a single vote at annual or special meetings of the credit union or co-operative. As a result, credit unions and co-operatives frequently refer to the concept of one member, one vote.

The second distinguishing feature is the business motivation of co-operative enterprises. Credit unions and co-operatives are not profit-maximizing organizations. Instead , their pricing strategy is developed to ensure that sufficient surplus is accumulated to ensure ongoing stability, but that excess profit is returned to the members through either dividends or user rebates, or (in the case of housing co-operatives) reduced housing charges.

Non-profit co-operatives are becoming increasingly important as a provider of basic necessities, such as housing, food, and child care. They tend to rely heavily on "volunteer" labour provided by their members, and in most non-profit co-operatives, each member is required to contribute a minimum number of hours of work per week or per month, in order to remain a member in good standing. A member of a non-profit co-operative may lose his rights or even his status as a member for persistent failure to contribute the required minimum number of hours ("non-participation"). In the case of a non-profit housing co-operative, a member may also be evicted from his housing unit for such non-participation.

Credit unions and caisses populaires are co-operative organizations and are established to serve member needs through the provision of a variety of financial services. Services include the taking of deposits and the making of loans to members at reasonable rates of interest. Unlike co-operatives, however, membership in credit unions is restricted, in some jurisdictions, to persons who have a common bond of occupation or association, or who reside in the same community.

¶ 3210   Organization

The organization of a co-operative, credit union, or caisse populaire is much like that of any other incorporated society. (*See Chapters 1 to 9, pages 3 to 37*).

¶ 3215   Liability of Members

The members are not responsible for the debts of the co-operative, credit union, or caisse populaire, except to the extent of any prohibited dividends or capital repayments received by them.

¶ 3220   Directors and Officers

The various co-operative corporation and credit union statutes (*see Appendix D, page 249*) set the minimum number of directors to be elected. The maximum number is unlimited. Most Acts require that a majority of directors be resident Canadians. Directors must be members, or directors, officers, shareholders, or members of a corporate member. The board of directors has the power and duty to manage the business and affairs of the corporation. (*See also Chapter 6, Directors, page 19.*)

In co-operatives and credit unions, officers are elected or appointed by the board of directors (*see also Chapter 7, Officers, page 25*).

¶ 3225   Committees

Every co-operative and credit union should have standing committees to assist the board of directors in managing the corporation. For example, most housing co-operatives have Membership, Financial, Maintenance, and Social committees. Other co-operatives and credit unions have committees tailored to their particular needs. (*See also Chapter 8, Committees, page 31, and Chapter 9, Committee of the Whole, page 37.*)

B.   Meetings of Members

¶ 3230   Notices of Meetings, and Agendas

The bylaws generally permit considerable flexibility in terms of how members are to be notified of an upcoming meeting. The bylaws may require that notices of each meeting be sent by mail to the address of the member. However, some bylaws permit notice of the meeting to be posted or published in a local newspaper. The bylaws also typically spell out how long in advance of the meeting notice must be sent out. There is typically a saving provision in the bylaws so that any resolution passed at a meeting is not invalid simply because there was some technical defect in delivering notice to the full membership.

The business to be conducted at a meeting should be set out in the notice of the meeting.

Some constitutions limit the co-operative or credit union to conducting only such business at the meeting as is set out in the notice of meeting. However, some statutes (e.g., the *Ontario Co-operative Corporations Act,* Section 77) permit members at an annual meeting to raise any matter relevant to the business and affairs of the co-operative If the constitution and the statute do not either prevent or compel the Chair to deal with business for which no prior notice has been given, the Chair should permit only minor or routine matters to be added to the agenda, under the heading "New Business". Any important matter for which no notice has been given should be dealt with at a future meeting or should be referred to the board of directors or to a committee (*see Rule 13.5, Adding to an Agenda, page 67.*)

¶ 3235   Quorum

(*See also Chapter 15, Quorum.*) Quorum requirements are usually set out in the bylaws. While some credit union and co-operative meetings are very large gatherings, unless there is some issue which has disturbed the membership, typically only a small percentage of the members attend the meeting. Prior to the meeting being called to order, it is essential that the bylaws be consulted to ensure that there is a quorum for the meeting. The existence of a quorum should be noted in the minutes of the meeting.

¶ 3240   Voting and Voting Principles

(*See also Chapter 22, Voting Methods, page 115, Chapter 23, Sense of the Meeting, page 123, and Chapter 24, Elections and Appointments, page 127.*) In a co-operative or credit union, each member has one vote. The only exception to this principle is in elections for the board of directors, in which each member has the number of votes equal to the number of candidates to be elected.

(i) Elections and Appointments

(*See also Chapter 24, Elections and Appointments, page 127.*) The "cumulative" and "ranking" methods of voting (referred to in Chapter 4, Voting Systems, page 13) are prohibited by some provincial co-operative and credit union statutes for elections to the board of directors (e.g.,

Ontario Co-operative Corporations Act, Section 91; *Ontario Credit Unions Act,* Section 44).

(ii) Voting on Motions

Motions are generally decided by a show of hands, unless a demand for a poll is made. The Chair cannot move or second a motion while occupying the chair, but he is entitled to vote on a motion. The Chair should, however, abstain from voting on a "quick vote" (show of hands, etc.) except in the event of a tie vote (*see Rule 10.8, Chair's Right at Meetings, page 48*). If the Chair has voted and a tie has resulted, the motion is lost. However, if the Chair has not voted, the Chair may then cast a vote to break the tie.

A "casting vote" exists only where a statute or a bylaw accords the Chair a second vote in order to break a tie. Generally speaking, credit unions and co-operatives do not accord the Chair a "casting vote". In the event that a tie exists, the motion is lost unless the Chair has not voted in the first instance and is prepared to break the tie by casting a single vote to break the tie.

It is up to the Chair to decide whether a motion has been carried, or in the case of a special resolution, whether it has been carried by the required majority. If nobody demands a poll, the Chair's decision as to whether a motion has been carried or not is determinative of the matter.

Sometimes, shares in a co-operative or credit union are held jointly. Generally, the bylaws of the credit union and the co-operative provide that joint shareholders have a single vote, and that if joint shareholders cannot agree as to how that vote is cast, it shall not be counted. Unincorporated associations may be members of credit unions or co-operatives, and generally, the bylaws of the co-operative or credit union provide that the president may vote on behalf of the unincorporated association. Incorporated societies may also be members of credit unions and co-operatives, and one of the directors or officers of the corporation appointed under its corporate seal may attend and vote on behalf of the corporation at meetings of members.

¶ 3245 Proxies

Most provincial co-operative and credit union statutes[1] prohibit members of co-operatives and credit unions from voting by proxy[2]. (*See Chapter 14, Proxies, page 69.*)

---

1 The *Ontario Co-operative Act* (sec. 76), and the *Ontario Credit Unions Act* (sec. 29), for example, both prohibit members from voting by proxy.

2 The *British Columbia Act* (sec. 63) permits a member to vote by proxy if he lives more than fifty miles away.

However, corporate members are permitted to appoint a director or officer to attend and vote on its behalf at meetings of members, and members of unincorporated associations may do the same (unless prohibited by the governing statute or the constitution).

In Manitoba, the Act limits the use of proxies: only members may be proxyholders, and then only for one member. The proxy is valid only for the designated meeting, and may be revoked at any time. The notice of meeting may require that proxies be filed up to forty-eight hours before the meeting.

For motions and amendments, see Chapter 17, Motions, page 83, and Chapter 18, Amendments to Motions, page 91.

For discussion and interrupting discussion, see Chapter 19, Discussion, page 97, Chapter 20, Interrupting Discussion — Procedural Motions, page 101, and Chapter 21, Interrupting Discussion — Demands, page 109.

¶ 3250   Annual Meetings

Annual meetings are especially important to credit unions and co-operatives. It is at the annual meeting that the board of directors is elected from the members, the dividend and user rebate is approved, the auditors are appointed, and the management reports on its activities in the previous year. Most importantly, it is at the annual meeting that members express their concerns about services which have been provided, and advance their recommendations to enhance the services of the credit union or co-operative. The effectiveness in advancing recommendations to the board of directors has resulted in a degree of responsiveness to member needs, which makes credit union and co-operative organizations attractive to their members.

The order of business for credit union and co-operative meetings is usually set out in the bylaws. Generally, the order of business for annual meetings (after the formal opening of the meeting — *see Chapter 16, Meetings of Members, page 77, and Appendix A, Forms S–10 and S–11, pages 209 to 210*) is as follows:

1. Reports of the Board of Directors.

2. Report of the Manager.

3. Reports of Committees.

4. Auditor's Report.

5. Election of Directors.

6. New Business.

¶ 3255 Special Meetings

At a special meeting of members (a meeting called to consider a specific important item of new business), the business at the meeting (after the opening formalities) may consist solely of the item which the meeting was called to consider.

¶ 3260 Requisitioned Meetings, Motions, and Circulated Statements

In many co-operatives and credit unions, the governing statute, the constitution, or the bylaws give the members a right to convene a meeting of members upon obtaining the signatures of a small percentage of the members on a "requisition" (petition). Such requisitioned meetings are becoming more common as members of co-operatives and credit unions become increasingly aware of their rights.

On occasion, members may feel that the board of directors has lost credibility and should be required to resign. Sometimes such dissatisfaction results in a motion of non-confidence in the board of directors. Such motions do not require the board to resign. Directors can only be removed from the board if the governing legislation and the rules of natural justice relating to the removal of directors are adhered to: i.e., by complying with notice requirements, by stating clearly in the notice of meeting that the meeting is being called to bring a motion to remove the directors, and by offering an opportunity for the directors to make representations at the meeting.

In some co-operatives and credit unions, members also have the right to require the board of directors:

(a) To give notice, to all members, of any motion that may properly be moved and is intended to be moved by any member at the next scheduled meeting of members, and;

(b) To circulate, to all members, a statement commenting on any proposed motion or any business to be dealt with at the next scheduled meeting of members.

The statute, constitution, or bylaw authorizing the requisitioned meeting, motion, or circulated statement must be strictly complied with.

¶ 3265   How to Run an Effective Meeting

(*See also Chapter 30, How to Conduct a Meeting of Members, page 159.*) Membership meetings provide an extraordinary opportunity for a one-on-one exchange between members of the credit union or co-operative, and those charged with its stewardship. The input provided by members is essential for management, staff, and the board of directors to ensure that they are going in an appropriate direction and setting realistic priorities. Meetings also provide an opportunity to attract new volunteers and to increase the credit union's or co-operative's public profile. Accordingly, to take full advantage of the platform that a membership meeting provides, the board of directors should more than satisfy basic legal requirements. They should highlight recent accomplishments, honour staff and active members, try to improve the social relationship between the members, staff, management, and the board of directors, renew and clarify policies on social and community neighbourhood involvement, and actively solicit the involvement of more volunteers to elected positions. Instead of merely reading a scripted annual report, the board should use audio-visual aids to enhance the report and to inform the members of important achievements and future directions.

Very often, credit union and co-operative meetings attract individuals who quite enjoy an opportunity to express themselves in front of a gathering. These people have a tendency to dominate the exchange of opinions, which can result in the meeting becoming far too focused and, at times, totally divergent from the agenda. One of the problems the Chair of the meeting has, is to continually show courtesy to the membership, but at the same time effectively control the meeting to ensure that no individual dominates the meeting excessively. It is essential that the Chair of the meeting be totally familiar with the rules of order governing the meeting, so that he can resolve procedural entanglements with finality.

Before each membership meeting, clear objectives should be agreed upon, and after the meeting, there should be an evaluation completed to ensure that those objectives have been achieved. Typical objectives might include:

1. Attracting more members to the meeting.

2. Conducting clear and concise presentations.

3. Encouraging good, two-way communication with particular emphasis on questions being asked.

4. Developing an effective audio-visual presentation.

5. Encouraging participation in the election procedure, preferably soliciting the involvement of new volunteers.

6. Leaving members with a sense of commitment to the organization and an understanding of its role and stability.

¶ 3270   Forms

See Appendix C, page 245, for Co-Operative Forms.

PART V

MISCELLANEOUS

CHAPTER 33

How to Start a Society

¶ 3300   General

A society can begin in many ways — spontaneously or by design. (In this work, "society" includes a club, an association, and any group of people or societies, whether or not incorporated). There is no single or simple formula; the procedure varies according to the circumstances, the people involved, and the aims of the group.

This chapter addresses itself to the starting up of a small society in its simplest form — grass roots — which can grow from a gathering of friends around someone's coffee table, to becoming a movement for public welfare or self interest, according to its aims. Many international political or social organizations began in this manner, some ending in revolution (as in Czarist Russia or the United States of America), some growing into international service organizations (like Kiwanis and Rotary Clubs and Red Cross), and some ending ignominiously in complete oblivion.

Most social clubs also begin this way, but some have to be revived (in the same manner) every year or two. The traditional international societies have well-established rules and procedures for starting up local branches or cells, and are prepared to render valuable assistance to the applicants as long as they concur with the spirit of the organization. However, the same result may be achieved by a group setting up its own society from scratch and then applying for admittance to the international organization as an established unit.

The following is a typical scenario for the formation of a "grass roots" organization:

(i) Preliminary Steps

1. There is at least one prime mover, instigator, or promoter who is prepared to stick his neck out to show an interest in a specific

195

topic. He gets his first adherent(s) by discussing his project with anyone who will listen. At the same time he looks for co-workers — people who will help him in the promotion and the operation of the organization.

2. This individual gathers around him a few others who have the same interest. They may be friends or acquaintances of his, or people who answered his telephone calls or his advertisements that he placed in the press or on sign boards in the schools, at work office bulletin boards, or on the street.

3. As soon as he begins to assemble supporters, he calls them together for a series of "brainstorming" sessions. These meetings are kept small and informal until it appears that the group is dedicated to the avowed purpose and is prepared to work for it. Naysayers are not welcome at this stage.

(ii) Preliminary Meetings

1. When it is felt that there is a nucleus for an organization, the first pre-organization meeting is called by personal invitation. Attention is focused on persons who whole-heartedly concur with the aims and purposes. Dissidents are avoided.

2. The first function of the pre-organization meeting is the selection of an interim Chair — someone to act as a traffic cop for the discussions — preferably a person with some experience in societies. The procedure for selecting a Chair as set out in Rule 10.4, Temporary Chair, may be followed, or, because there may not be many members as yet, the Chair may be self-selected.

   At this stage, permanent committees and committee Chair and officers need not be appointed. It is advisable to wait until the purposes of the organization have been crystallized and a nucleus of compatible, dedicated people has been assembled. Instead, for the time being, everyone may be considered a member of every committee. Discussions should be conducted in the style of "committees of the whole" (*Chapter 9, Committee of the Whole, page 37*).

3. The following topics are discussed at pre-organization meetings (there may be one or more):

   (a) goals: crystallizing the purposes and aims of the proposed organization, and preparing a memorandum that lays out the purposes and aims of the organization. The exact wording of the purposes and aims of the organization may become most important in the future, therefore careful attention should be paid to them at this stage. It is much easier to make changes now than after the society has been organized.

The memorandum outlining the discussions which took place at the pre-organization meetings is prepared by a person previously designated. It should indicate who will be invited to join the society, how it may be funded, and any other recommendations and suggestions.

(b) membership: methods of increasing membership, such as word-of-mouth, posters , advertising, etc. A person, preferably one who has many contacts in his work or in his private life, is selected to temporarily lead discussions to consider procedures for increasing membership — whether or not to go after "big names" or persons whose presence will add prestige to the organization, for example.

A summary of these discussions is prepared by a previously designated person for use at the first general meeting. If any decisions are made, they must be noted.

(c) finances: methods of raising funds. A person, preferably one with some financing or business experience (e.g., a bank employee, a bookkeeper, or an accountant) is asked to look after finances — maybe act as interim treasurer. The group decides upon funding sources — whether to rely on self-imposed dues, to seek public support or government aid, or to seek out other sources.

Caution should be exercised regarding expenses. Whoever incurs an expense for printing, advertising, rent, etc. may become personally responsible to the creditor for the amount of the entire debt. A specific trust fund should be opened and contributions collected for these purposes.

The meeting may investigate and recommend whether the society should require an initiation fee for everyone joining, as well as a regular annual (or monthly) membership fee. It will be up to the first (or subsequent) meeting after the society is organized, to pass on the recommendation.

4. By this time, a healthy nucleus has been assembled — people who are interested in the purposes and aims of the proposed society and who are prepared to work to accomplish its purposes and aims. An organization meeting may now be held. Whether the invitations are wide open or restricted depends on the circumstances.

(iii) First Meeting of Members

The following are suggestions for the agenda for the organization meeting:

1. Agenda (Part I) — Preliminary Matters

    (a) appointing a Chair: the organizer usually takes the chair and acts as Chair until the society, at a duly called general meeting, later appoints a permanent Chair.

    (b) welcome: the Chair (organizer) introduces and welcomes the people attending the meeting, including guests.

    (c) appointing a secretary: a secretary is appointed by the Chair or the meeting to take notes for the preparation of minutes of the meeting.

    (d) attendance record: the secretary should have everyone sign an attendance sheet or attendance slips indicating names, addresses, phone numbers, and special interests. An attendance sheet may be passed around during the meeting, or attendance slips may be handed out at the beginning of the meeting and collected during the meeting or on the way out.

    (e) goals: the Chair (organizer) outlines the purposes and aims of the society. Members and guests may be given the floor to talk about the background of the society, its organization, and its future directions.

    Copies of the memorandum referred to in (ii) 3.(a), above may be distributed at this stage.

2. Agenda (Part II) — Organizing the Society

    (a) name: settling on a name for the society (refer to the memorandum).

    (b) constitution: appointing a special committee to draft a constitution to be considered at the next meeting of members.

    (c) membership: considering having conditions of membership (if desired): qualifications, training, expertise, special interest, etc.; and considering ways of increasing membership.

    (d) fees, dues: considering methods of raising funds for the purpose of the society, appointing a special committee to report back to the next general meeting with recommendations on whether an initiation fee for joining is advisable, and suggesting the amount of the annual (or monthly) dues; investigating grants (government, community and foundation, parent body, etc.); seeking out private donors.

(e) publicity: if it is a requirement of or a benefit to the society, appointing a person or committee to organize a public relations campaign.

3. Agenda (Part III) — Elections

It would be wise not to rush the election of permanent officers. It takes time to assess the capability and compatibility of prospective officers.

Operating for a while on an informal basis will give the members and potential members and officers an opportunity to ascertain how deeply they feel about the society and its aims, and what each is capable of contributing.

4. Agenda (Part IV) — Ending the Meeting

Discuss and decide on the date and place of the next meeting, or the schedule of subsequent meetings.

Declare the meeting concluded.

Good luck!

CHAPTER 34

Advice to an Inexperienced Chair

¶ 3400   General

1. The Chair must be

- patient;

- knowledgeable of the constitution and the rules of order, and be ready and willing to enforce them;

- firm, fair, and fearless in his decisions (fearless enough to be unpopular with those who disagree with his decisions);

- impartial on all questions: fair to the majority, and protecting their interests if they are silent, but also fair to the minority, and protecting minority interests;

- tactful and diplomatic;

- sensitive to everyone's feelings.

As well, the Chair must

- be familiar with the constitution and the rules (he may have a parliamentarian advise him during the meeting);

- should have before him a copy of the Rules of Order adopted by the society (see ¶ 320, Adoption of Rules of Order, page 12);

- be prepared to determine, with respect to every motion made

  — whether a speaker can be interrupted

  — whether the discussion can be interrupted

  — whether it is debatable

  — whether it is amendable

  — what majority it requires

— what precedence it has over other motions

— to what motions it can be applied

— whether it can be renewed, if lost

— whether it can be appealed (*see chart, inside front cover*)

• bring out the best in every speaker, especially one who is timid;

• check or suppress an unnecessarily talkative speaker;

• know his material (he should not have to shuffle through papers to get the desired information);

• know when to close the meeting. The meeting should not be dragged out after the business for which it was called is concluded.

2. The Chair must not

• rule a member "out of order" without giving him an explanation;

• refuse to carry out his duties, when presented with a motion to which he is opposed;

• be autocratic, dictatorial, or dogmatic, nor impose his opinions on the meeting;

• carry on private conversations or asides with members, or permit others to do so;

• leave the chair without appointing a temporary Chair or recessing the meeting;

• let the meeting run on and on (once every item has been covered, he must close the meeting);

• allow members to attack each other personally.

Appendix A

Forms for Society Meetings

Forms for Condominiums
    See Appendix B, page 239

Forms for Co-operatives
    See Appendix C, page 245

FORM S–1

Notice of Annual Meeting

[*NAME OF SOCIETY*]

NOTICE OF ANNUAL MEETING OF MEMBERS

TAKE NOTICE that the annual meeting of members of the [*name of Society*] will be held at [*place*] on [*date*] at [*time*], for the purpose of

(a) receiving[1], considering, and approving the financial statement for the past fiscal year, together with the auditors' report thereon, and all the transactions reflected thereby;

(b) electing directors;

(c) appointing auditors, and authorizing the board of directors to fix their remuneration;

(d) considering and dealing with a proposed motion to ....; and

(e) transacting such other business as may properly come before the meeting.

[*If proxies are permitted, add:*]

Members who will not be attending the meeting are requested to date, sign, and return the accompanying proxy in the envelope provided for that purpose.

Only members in good standing are entitled to attend, participate, and vote at the meeting.

[*Add, if applicable:*]

Accompanying this notice is a letter explaining the proposed motion.

DATED..

On behalf of the board of directors

A.B., Secretary

FORM S–2

Notice of Special Meeting

[*NAME OF SOCIETY*]

NOTICE OF SPECIAL MEETING OF MEMBERS

TAKE NOTICE that a special meeting of the members of the [*name of Society*] will be held at [*place*] on [*date*] at [*time*], for the purpose of considering, and if thought fit, confirming with or without such variation or amendment as may be made at the meeting,

---

[1] If management does not seek the approval of the financial statement, use

"Receiving and considering the financial statement for the past fiscal year, together with the auditors' report thereon."

(a) a special resolution passed by the board on [*date*], which reads as follows: [*set out resolution in full*];

(b) a special resolution passed by the board on [*date*], a copy of which is annexed hereto and forms part of this notice;

(c) a resolution of the board passed on [*date*] for [*indicate purpose of resolution*], and to take such action thereon as may be deemed proper. The said resolution reads as follows:
.... [*or*, A copy of the said resolution is annexed hereto and forms part of this notice]; or

(d) Bylaw No. .... authorizing the sale of the assets and the undertaking of the Society to ...., on the terms set out in the draft agreement annexed to the said bylaw. A copy of this bylaw and agreement accompany this notice.

Members who will not be attending the meeting are requested to date, sign, and return the accompanying proxy in the envelope provided for that purpose.

Accompanying this notice is a letter explaining the proposed motion (*or* motions).

DATED...

On behalf of the board of directors
A.B., Secretary

FORM S–3

Notice of Adjourned Meeting
[*NAME OF SOCIETY*]
NOTICE OF ADJOURNED MEETING OF MEMBERS

To the members
NAME OF SOCIETY

TAKE NOTICE that the annual [*or* special] meeting of members of the [*name of Society*], called for [*date*], has been adjourned to [*place*] on [*date*] at [*time*].

DATED ....

By order of the board
A.B., Secretary

FORM S–4

Notice of Board Meeting
[*NAME OF SOCIETY*]
NOTICE OF MEETING OF DIRECTORS

TAKE NOTICE that a meeting of the board of directors of the [*name of Society*] will be held at [*place*] on [*date*], the .... day of .... at [*time*].

DATED ....

By order of the president

....
(*Secretary*)

FORM S-5

Waiver of Notice of Meeting of Members

[NAME OF SOCIETY]

WAIVER OF NOTICE OF ANNUAL [*or* SPECIAL] MEETING

of the [*name of Society*]

I hereby waive notice of the time, place, and purpose of an annual [*or* special] meeting of members of the [*name of Society*], to be held on [*date*] at [*place*], and do hereby consent to the holding of such meeting.

DATED ....

* ....

(Signature)

FORM S-6

Waiver of Notice of Meeting of the Board

[NAME OF SOCIETY]

WAIVER OF NOTICE OF MEETING OF THE BOARD

We, the undersigned directors of the [*name of Society*] hereby waive notice of and consent to the holding of a meeting of the board of directors of the [*name of Society*] at [*place*] on [*date*] at [*time*], and agree to ratify all the resolutions passed and the business transacted thereat.

DATED ....

....

(Signature)

FORM S-7

Declaration of Service of Notice of Meeting

CANADA	)	
	)	IN THE MATTER OF [*name of Society*]
PROVINCE OF	)	
	)	
	)	AND IN THE MATTER OF
	)	the annual [*or* special] meeting
	)	thereof to be held on [*date*]
	)	
	)	

I, ..., of the City of ....
in the County of ...., solemnly
declare that

1. I am the .... of the [*name of Society*] and as
   such have knowledge of the matters herein set out.

2. I did, before the hour of 4:00 p.m. on [*date*], mail by first class ordinary mail, postage
   prepaid, to all members in good standing of the [*name of Society*] at their respective
   addresses appearing on the register of members as of [*date*], and to the auditors,
   Messrs. A, B, & C, the following documents:

   (a) notice of the annual [*or* special] meeting of the members of the [*name of Society*]
       (marked Schedule "A" hereto);

   (b) letter explaining the proposed motion (marked Schedule "B" hereto);

   (c) proxyform (marked Schedule "C" hereto);

   (d) annual report for the year ended [*date*] (marked Schedule "D" hereto);

   (e) return envelope (marked Schedule "E" hereto).

AND I make this solemn declaration, conscientiously believing it to be true, and
knowing that it is of the same force and effect as if made under oath.

DECLARED before me at the ....)
....)
of ....)
)
in the .... of.......................)
....)
this .... day of ....)
................................., 19......)
A Commissioner, etc.

FORM S–8

Proxyform

[*NAME OF SOCIETY*]

PROXYFORM

The undersigned member of the [*name of Society*] hereby appoints ....
or failing him, ..., or in lieu of the foregoing ....,
as proxyholder of the undersigned, to attend, act, and vote for and on behalf of the
undersigned at the annual [*or* special] meeting of members to be held on the ....
(including adjournments thereof), and hereby revokes all proxies previously given.

[Any of Form S–8, 1. to 5., below, may be added here.]

DATED ....

....
(*Signature*)

1. The said proxyholders are authorized and directed to vote for the election of
    .... and .... and ....
    as directors.

2. The said proxyholders are hereby restricted from voting for the election of
    .... and .... as directors.

3. The said proxyholders are authorized and directed to vote for the election of
    .... and .... as directors,
    and such others, if any, as they in their absolute discretion deem advisable.

4. The said proxyholders are authorized and directed to vote (with or without amend-
    ment) for [*or* against] the confirmation of Bylaw No. ....

5. The said proxyholders are authorized and directed to vote (with or without amend-
    ment) for [*or* against] the confirmation of the special resolution to [*describe resolu-
    tion*].

FORM S–9

Revocation of Proxy

To the [*name of Society*], and to the Chair of the Meeting

I hereby revoke the appointment of [*name*] as my proxyholder with respect to the
annual meeting of members of the [*name of Society*] to be held on [*date*].

DATED ....

....
(*Signature of member*)

FORM S–10

Agenda for Annual Meeting of Members

(See also Form S–11, Chair's Agenda for Annual Meeting)

1. Opening the meeting; registration of members.

2. Chair: Introduction or appointment.[2]

3. Secretary: Introduction or designation.

4. Scrutineers: appointment.

5. Introduction of guests.

6. Proof of mailing of notice.

7. Report on attendance, including proxies, if authorized.

---

[2] *In smaller societies and at round-table style meetings, some of the opening formalities may be
dispensed with (particularly the introduction of the officers).* There is no point in introducing the Chair
and the secretary if everyone present knows them, nor is there any need to give a report on attendance
when proxies are not permitted and all members are in sight of one another.

8. Verification of minutes of previous annual meeting (if required under the bylaws).

9. Approval of agenda; business arising from the minutes.

10. Report of the board of directors and/or the manager (Annual Report).

11. Report of the treasurer, financial statement.

12. Budget for the current year.

13. Reports of standing committees.

14. Reports of special committees.

15. Election of directors, (*or*, election of directors and officers, if applicable).

16. Appointment of auditors.

17. New business for which due notice has been given.

18. New business for which prior notice is not required.

19. Conclusion of meeting.

FORM S–11

Chair's Agenda for Annual Meeting

[*NAME OF SOCIETY*]

Annual Meeting held on [*date*]

CHAIR'S AGENDA

1. Opening the meeting (*see Chapter 16, Meetings of Members, page 77*):

    (a) "Order please. The meeting will now come to order."

    (b) "This is the annual meeting of [*name of Society*]."

    (c) "Has everyone registered with the secretary (*or* scrutineers) at the door? If not, would you please do so now?" *or* "We shall now have a roll call. Mr. Secretary, would you please call the roll?"

    (d) (*If proxies are permitted*) "Have all proxies been handed in? If not, please do so now."

2. Chair: introduction or appointment of the Chair:

    (a) If the person designated by the bylaws is taking the Chair, no introduction is necessary.

    (b) If the president (or the person designated by the bylaws) is not available "As the president is not available, I, as vice-president, will take the chair."

    (c) If no person designated by the bylaws is available, use Form S–11A to elect a Chair of the meeting.

3. Secretary: introduction or designation (or appointment) of the secretary of the meeting (*see Rule 16.4, Appointing a Secretary, page 78*):

    (a) "Mr. S. (the secretary of the society) will act as secretary of the meeting."

    (b) If the secretary of the meeting is to be appointed by the meeting, use Form S–11B.

210

Forms for Society Meetings

4. Scrutineers: appointment of scrutineers:

   (a) "If the meeting has no objection, I appoint Mr. T. and Mr. U as scrutineers to assist the Chair in the counting of votes (and proxies)."

   (b) If scrutineers are to be appointed by the meeting, use Form S–11C.

5. Introduction of guests (non-members):

   (a) Guests may be introduced to the meeting with brief comments.

   (b) By a simple majority of votes, the meeting may decide to exclude non-members from the meeting, or any part thereof. (*See Rule 11.2, Control of the Meeting, page 52.*)

   (c) The Society's auditor has the right to attend general meetings of the Society.

6. Proof of mailing notice:

   (a) "The notice calling the meeting was mailed to all the members of record (and others to whom notice is required to be sent) in accordance with the bylaws. A declaration to that effect is on file here for your perusal."

   (b) "Additional copies of the notice are available here if wanted."

7. Report on attendance (including proxies, if authorized):

   (a) "The scrutineers (*or* the secretary) reports on the attendance as follows:

   Members attending in person: . . . members

   Acceptable proxies representing: . . . members

   TOTAL in person and by proxy . . . members"

   (If the report is not ready, it may be read later).

   (b) "The Chair is advised that there is a quorum present, although the report on attendance is not yet ready. In the meantime, we will proceed with the meeting."

   (c) If the Chair does not adopt the secretary's (or the scrutineers') report on attendance: "The Chair has perused the attendance list and all the proxies questioned by the scrutineers, and declares that the attendance at this meeting is as follows: (*read the report as in 7(a) above*). There is a quorum present."

8. Verification of minutes of previous annual meeting (if required under the bylaws):

   "The minutes of the previous annual meeting of the society are available for perusal. Unless someone wishes them read, the Chair will entertain a motion to take the minutes as read and verified."

9. Approval of agenda (*see Chapter 13, Agendas, page 65*):

   (a) "A copy of the agenda was mailed with the notice of this meeting. (*or* was handed to you as you entered). Will someone make a motion approving the agenda as circulated (*or* a motion proposing any amendments desired)?"

   To approve — see Rule 13.3 at page 66.

   To renumber the items — see Rule 13.4 at page 66.

   To add items — see Rule 13.5 at page 67.

   To make an item a "special order" — see Rule 13.6 at page 68.

(b) After each motion has been moved and seconded, stated by the Chair and discussed (*see Chapter 17, Motions, page 83*), it should be read and voted on. The result of the voting should be announced. If the agenda was amended, the changes should be announced.

(c) "Is there any business arising from the minutes of the previous annual meeting?" (If so, it should be added to the agenda.)

10. Report of the board of directors and/or the officers (Annual Report):

(a) "You received a copy of the Annual Report with the notice of this meeting. Would the president (*or the general manager*) introduce the Annual Report and follow up with a motion to adopt it?. During the discussion on the motion, the members will have the opportunity to question the officers in connection with the report."

(b) "The Chair will entertain a motion to receive and approve the Annual Report."

11. Report of the treasurer (financial statement — unless combined with the Annual Report and approved. Same as 10, above.

12. Budget for the current year: "The treasurer will now introduce the proposed budget for the current year. Copies were distributed (*or copies are available at the head table*). After his introduction, he will move that the proposed budget for the current financial year be adopted. He will explain all the items and you will then be able to ask questions on it."

13. Reports of standing committees (*see Rule 8.7, Reports of Committees, page 35*):

(a) "The report of the Membership Committee was included in the Annual Report. If there are any questions, Mr. T, Chair of the committee will be pleased to answer them. Any questions?"

(b) "The report of the Building Committee will be read by Mr. U, its Chair. If you have any questions, he will be pleased to answer them. Any questions?"

(c) "The report of the Sports Committee was handed to you as you entered. If you have any questions, Mr. V, its Chair will be pleased to answer them. Any questions?"

(d) If it is the practice of the Society to accept, or adopt, or approve the reports of the standing committees, the relevant motion should be made. (*see Rule 17.3, Procedural Motions, page 85*).

14. Reports of special committees. (*see Rule 8.7, Reports of Committees, page 35*): Use the same procedure as for standing committees (above) If it is the final report of the special committee, the motion should include a provision dismissing the committee (and thanking the members for their work).

15. Election of directors (*See Chapter 6, Directors, page 19*) (*or election of directors and officers, if applicable*).

(a) If directors are to be elected by a single ballot (no contest) and the bylaws require a ballot, use Form S–11E.

(b) If the election of directors is contested, use Form S–11F.

(c) If directors and officers are to be elected by the members (as in the case of a direct model of society (*see ¶ 105(i), page 4*), use Forms S–11E and S–11F, page 215.

16. Appointment of auditor (*see Chapter 7, Officers, page 25*): "The Chair will now entertain a motion for the appointment of an auditor." Use Form S–11G.

17. New business for which due notice has been given (*see Chapter 17, Motions, page 83*): "Included in the notice of this annual meeting was a notice of a Special Resolution to . . ., which your board of directors would like to present to you for your consideration. Mr. D. will move its approval."

18. New business for which prior notice is not required: "Is there any new business the meeting would like to discuss that does not require specific notice?"

19. Conclusion of meeting (*see Chapter 26, Closing the Meeting, page 139*):

    (a) "As there is no further business, the meeting is concluded."

    (b) "As there is no further business, the Chair will entertain a motion to conclude the meeting."

FORM S–11A — Election of Chair

A temporary Chair is first appointed informally by the meeting (*see Rule 11.5, Ordinary Meetings, page 53*).

Temporary Chair:

(a) "In the absence of the president and the vice-president, and with your consent, I will act as temporary Chair and conduct an election for the permanent Chair of the meeting."

(b) "The meeting is now open for nominations for Chair."[3]

[*Nominations are made.*]

(c) "Are there any further nominations?"

(d) "As only one person[3] has been nominated, may I have a motion to declare Mr. C elected Chair of the meeting?"[4]

(e) "Moved by Mr. M, seconded by Mr. N, that Mr. C be elected Chair of this meeting. All those in favour, please signify in the usual manner by raising the right hand. Contrary, if any? Carried (unanimously). I declare Mr. C elected Chair of this meeting."

(f) "I will now retire. Will Mr. C please take the chair?"

FORM S–11B — Appointment of Secretary

(a) "The meeting is now open for a motion to appoint a secretary."

(b) "It has been moved by Mr. M, seconded by Mr. N, that Mr. S be appointed secretary of this meeting. All those in favour please signify in the usual manner by raising the right hand. Contrary, if any? Carried (unanimously)."[5]

---

[3] If more than one is nominated and a poll is demanded, use Form S–11D.

[4] Or he may be declared elected by acclamation.

[5] If the motion is defeated, substitute:

    (d) "The motion is defeated. May I have another motion to appoint?" [*Proceed with* (a), (b), *and* (c) *until a motion appointing a secretary is carried successfully.*]

FORM S–11C — Appointment of Scrutineers

(a) "Would the meeting like to appoint scrutineers? The Chair will receive a motion to that effect."

Motion: "Resolved that Mr. T and Mr. U be appointed scrutineers."

(b) "It has been moved by Mr. M, seconded by Mr. N, that Mr. T and Mr. U be appointed scrutineers of the meeting. All those in favour, please signify in the usual manner by raising the right hand. Contrary, if any? Carried (unanimously)."[6]

FORM S–11D — Demand for a Poll

(a) "As a poll has been demanded [*or*, is required], the scrutineers will please distribute ballots, and the secretary will give instructions in the use of the ballots."

Secretary:

"If you are in favour of the motion, mark an "X" in the box opposite the word "FOR". If you are against the motion, mark an "X" in the box opposite the word "AGAINST". Then sign your name clearly. If you are a proxyholder for absent members, indicate clearly how you are instructed to vote the shares of the members whom you represent."

(b) "Will the scrutineers now collect the ballots?"

(c) "Are all the ballots in the hands of the scrutineers? If so, the scrutineers will now retire to count the ballots and report back to the Chair."

[*The scrutineers retire and count the ballots. As soon as they are ready, they report to the Chair in writing on Form S–23, S–24, S–25, or S–26. The meeting may be recessed or adjourned while the scrutineers are counting the ballots. When the scrutineers have reported, proceed with the meeting.*]

(d) "Order. The meeting will now come to order. The Chair has received the scrutineers' report. It reads as follows": [*Chair reads the report and considers its acceptance.*]

(e) "The Chair adopts the report of the scrutineers and declares the motion carried" [*or* defeated, *as the case may be*].[7]

---

[6] If the motion is defeated, substitute:

    (d) "The motion is defeated. May I have another motion to appoint?" [*Proceed with* (a), (b) *and* (c) *until a motion appointing scrutineers is carried successfully.*]

[7] If the Chair does not adopt the scrutineers' report, substitute:

    (e) "The Chair does not adopt the scrutineers' report. The Chair has examined all the ballots cast and the proxies on which the count is based and declares the result of the poll as follows:

    FOR ....

    AGAINST ....

    The Chair declares the motion carried" [*or* defeated, *as the case may be*].

FORM S–11E — Election of Directors by Single Ballot (Uncontested)

(a) As the bylaws require that the election of directors be by ballot, the Chair will receive a motion directing the secretary to cast a single ballot for the election of the persons nominated:

"Resolved that the secretary be directed to cast a single ballot on behalf of those present at the meeting for the election of the persons nominated as directors."

(b) "You have heard the motion by [*name of mover*] and seconded by [*name of seconder*]. [*No discussion on this motion.*] All in favour, signify in the usual manner. Any against? Carried (unanimously)."

(c) "Will the secretary please cast a ballot as directed?"

[*Secretary prepares and casts ballot.*]

(d) "I declare ....
elected directors of the Society by ballot, to hold office until their successors are duly elected or appointed."

FORM S–11F — Election of Directors (Contested)

(a) "Are there any further nominations? Will someone move that nominations be closed?":

"Resolved that nominations be closed."

(b) "You have heard the motion by [*name of mover*] and seconded by [*name of seconder*]. All in favour, indicate by raising the right hand. Any against? Carried (unanimously)."

(c) "The following have been nominated: Mr. A, B, C, D, E, and F."

(d) "The scrutineers will distribute ballots, and the secretary will give instructions for the use of the ballots."

Secretary:

"You will mark an "X" opposite the names of the persons of your choice.[8] You may vote for less than the required number, but not for more. You need not vote for the entire slate of candidates of one group. Sign your name clearly and indicate whether you are casting all your votes as proxy in the same manner."

(e) "Will the scrutineers now collect the ballots?"

(f) "Are all the ballots in the hands of the scrutineers? If so, the scrutineers will now retire to count the ballots and report back to the Chair."

[*The scrutineers retire and count the ballots. As soon as they are ready, they report to the Chair in writing as in Forms S–24 or S–25. The Chair may recess or adjourn the meeting while the scrutineers are counting the ballots. On receipt of the report, proceed with the meeting.*]

---

[8] If the ballots do not contain the names of all the candidates, substitute:

Secretary:

"You will print on the ballot the names of the persons for whose election you wish to vote. Only persons who have been nominated and whose names have been read by the Chair may be voted for. The names of not more than [*five*] are to be inserted in the ballot. Be sure to sign your name clearly at the foot of the ballot and indicate whether you are casting all your votes as proxy in the same manner."

(g) "The meeting will now come to order. The Chair has received the scrutineers' report which reads as follows": [*reads report*].

(h) "The Chair adopts the report of the scrutineers[9] and declares .... duly elected directors of the Society, to hold office until their successors are duly elected or appointed."

FORM S–11G — Election of Officers (Direct Model of Organization)

(a) "Are there any further nominations for president? Are there any further nominations for vice-president? Will someone move that nominations be closed?"

"Resolved that nominations be closed."

(b) "You have heard the motion by [*name of mover*] and seconded by [*name of seconder*]. All in favour, indicate by raising your right hand. Any against? Carried (unanimously)."

(c) "The following persons have been nominated:

For president: A and B

For vice-president: C and D."

(d) "The scrutineers will distribute ballots, and the secretary will give instructions for the use of the ballots."

Secretary:

"You will mark an "X" opposite the names of the persons of your choice.[10] Sign your name clearly and indicate whether you are casting all your votes as proxy in the same manner."

(e) "Will the scrutineers now collect the ballots?"

(f) "Are all of the ballots in the hands of the scrutineers? If so, the scrutineers will now retire to count the ballots and report back to the Chair."

---

[9] If the Chair does not adopt the report of the scrutineers, substitute:

"The Chair does not adopt the scrutineers' report. The Chair has examined all the ballots and the proxies on which the count is based and declares the result of the balloting as follows:

A ....

B ....

C ....

D ....

E ....

The Chair therefore declares .... to be duly elected directors of the Society, to hold office until their successors are duly elected or appointed."

[10] If the ballots do not contain the names of all the candidates, substitute:

Secretary:

"You will print on the ballot the names of the persons for whose election you wish to vote. Only persons who have been nominated and whose names have been read by the Chair may be voted for. You have one vote for president and one vote for vice-president. If you are voting by proxy, print the name of your appointor at the bottom of the ballot, followed by the words "by proxy" and then sign the ballot in your own name."

[*The scrutineers retire and count the ballots. The Chair may recess or adjourn the meeting while the scrutineers are counting the ballots. As soon as they are ready, they report to the Chair in writing as in Form S–25. On receipt of the report, the meeting may be proceeded with*].

(g) "The meeting will now come to order. The Chair has received the scrutineers' report which reads as follows": [*reads report*].

(h) "The Chair adopts the report of the scrutineers[11] and declares A elected as president and D elected as vice-president of the Society, to hold office until their successors are duly elected or appointed."

FORM S–12

Agenda for Ordinary Meeting of Members

1. Opening the meeting: registration of members.
2. Chair: introduction or appointment.[12]
3. Officials: introduction or designation of secretary, scrutineers and other officials.
4. Proof of mailing of notice.
5. Report on attendance, including proxies, if authorized.
6. Verification of minutes of previous meeting.
7. Approval of agenda; business arising from minutes.
8. Reports, if any.
9. New business for which due notice has been given.
10. New business for which prior notice is not required.
11. Conclusion of meeting.

---

[11] If the Chair does not adopt the report of the scrutineers, substitute:

"The Chair does not adopt the scrutineers' report. The Chair has examined all the ballots and the proxies on which the court is based and declares the result of the balloting as follows:

For president:

    A: .... votes

    B: .... votes

For vice-president:

    C: .... votes

    D: .... votes

The Chair therefore declares A elected as president and D as vice-president of the Society, to hold office until their successors are duly elected or appointed."

[12] *In smaller societies and at round-table style meetings, some of the opening formalities may be dispensed with (particularly the introduction of the officers).* There is no point in introducing the Chair and the secretary if everyone present knows them, nor is there any need to give a report on attendance when proxies are not permitted and all members are in sight of one another.

FORM S–13

Chair's Agenda for Ordinary Meeting

[*NAME OF SOCIETY*]

Meeting held on [*date*]

CHAIR'S AGENDA

1. Opening the meeting (*see Chapter 16, Meetings of Members, page 77*):

   (a) "Order please. The meeting will now come to order."

   (b) "This is an ordinary order meeting of [*name of Society*]."

   (c) "Has everyone registered with the secretary (*or* scrutineers) at the door? If not, would you please do so now?" *or* "We shall now have a roll call. Mr. Secretary, would you please call the roll"

   (d) (*If proxies are permitted*) "Have all proxies been handed in? If not, please do so now."

2. Chair: introduction or appointment of the Chair:

   (a) If the person designated by the bylaws is taking the Chair, no introduction is necessary.

   (b) If the president (or the person designated by the bylaws) is not available: "As the president is not available, I, as vice-president, will take the chair."

   (c) If no person designated by the bylaws is available, use Form S–11A to elect a Chair of the meeting.

3. Secretary: introduction or designation (or appointment) of the secretary of the meeting (*see Rule 16.4, Appointing a Secretary, page 78*):

   (a) "Mr. S. (the secretary of the society) will act as secretary of the meeting."

   (b) If the secretary of the meeting is to be appointed by the meeting, use Form S–11B.

4. Scrutineers: appointment of scrutineers:

   (a) "If the meeting has no objection, I appoint Mr. T. and Mr. U as scrutineers to assist the Chair in the counting of votes (and proxies)."

   (b) If scrutineers are to be appointed by the meeting, use Form S–11C.

5. Proof of mailing notice: (Form S–7):

   (a) "The notice calling the meeting was mailed to all the members of record (and others to whom notice is required to be sent) in accordance with the bylaws. A declaration to that effect is on file here for your perusal."

   (b) "Additional copies of the notice are available here if wanted."

6. Report on attendance (including proxies, if authorized):

   (a) The scrutineers (*or* the secretary) reports on the attendance as follows:

   Members attending in person: . . . members

   Acceptable proxies representing: . . . members

   TOTAL in person and by proxy . . . members"

(If the report is not ready, it may be read later).

(b) "The Chair is advised that there is a quorum present, although the report on attendance is not yet ready. In the meantime, we will proceed with the meeting."

(c) If the Chair does not adopt the secretary's (or the scrutineers') report on attendance: "The Chair has perused the attendance list and all the proxies questioned by the scrutineers, and declared that the attendance at this meeting is as follows: (*read the report as in 6(a) above*). There is a quorum present."

7. Verification of minutes of previous meeting (if required under the bylaws): see Rule 16.8, Verification of Minutes, page 79: "The minutes of the previous meeting of the society are available for perusal. Unless someone wishes them read, the Chair will entertain a motion to take the minutes as read and verified."

8. Approval of agenda (*see Chapter 13, Agendas, page 65*):

(a) "A copy of the agenda was mailed with the notice of this meeting. (*or* was handed to you as you entered). Will someone make a motion approving the agenda as circulated" (*or* a motion proposing any amendments desired)?

To approve — see Rule 13.3 at page 66.

To renumber the items — see Rule 13.4 at page 66.

To add items — see Rule 13.5 at page 67.

To make an item a "special order" — see Rule 13.6 at page 68.

(b) After each motion has been moved and seconded (*see Chapter 17, Motions, page 83*), stated by the Chair and discussed (*see Chapter 19, Discussion, page 97*), it should be read and voted on. The result of the voting should be announced. If the agenda was amended, the voting should be announced. If the agenda was amended, the changes should be announced.

(c) "Is there any business arising from the minutes of the previous meeting?" (If so, it should be added to the agenda.)

9. Special business for which the meeting was called:

(a) "Included in the notice of this meeting was a notice of a special motion to (*describe new business*). This motion requires a (two-thirds) majority." "Mr. T. has a motion to . . . He will move the motion and explain it. Is there a seconder?"

(b) "Moved by Mr. T., seconded by Mr. U. "RESOLVED that . . . (*the Chair or the secretary reads the motion*). Is there any discussion on the motion?" (After discussion has ended, including the mover's reply, the motion should be put to a vote. Follow the procedure as in 8(b), above.)

10. New business for which prior notice is not required: "Is there any new business the meeting would like to discuss that does not require specific notice?"

11. Conclusion of meeting (*see Chapter 26, Closing the Meeting, page 139*):

(a) "That concludes the business of the meeting. Therefore the meeting is concluded. Thank you."

(b) "That concludes the business of the meeting, the Chair will now entertain a motion to conclude the meeting. Thank you."

FORM S–14

Agenda for Special Meeting of Members

1. Opening the meeting: registration of members.
2. Chair: introduction or appointment.[13]
3. Officials: introduction or designation of secretary, scrutineers and other officials.
4. Proof of mailing of notice.
5. Report on attendance, including proxies, if authorized.
6. Verification of minutes of previous meeting.
7. Approval of agenda.
8. Special business for which the meeting was called. Motion, seconding, amendments, discussion, reply, vote.
9. Conclusion of meeting.

FORM S–15

Chair's Agenda for Special Meeting

1. Opening the meeting (*see Chapter 16, Meetings of Members, page 77*):

   (a) "Order please. The meeting will now come to order."

   (b) "This is an ordinary meeting of [*name of Society*]."

   (c) "Has everyone registered with the secretary (*or* scrutineers) at the door? If not, would you please do so now?" *or* "We shall now have a roll call. Mr. Secretary, would you please call the roll?"

   (d) (*If proxies are permitted*) "Have all proxies been handed in? If not, please do so now."

2. Chair: introduction or appointment of the Chair:

   (a) If the person designated by the bylaws is taking the Chair, no introduction is necessary.

   (b) If the president (or the person designated by the bylaws) is not available: "As the president is not available, I, as vice-president, will take the chair."

   (c) If no person designated by the bylaws is available, use Form S–11A to elect a Chair of the meeting.

3. Secretary: introduction or designation (or appointment) of the secretary of the meeting (*see Rule 16.4, Appointing a Secretary, page 78*):

   (a) "Mr. S. (the secretary of the society) will act as secretary of the meeting."

   (b) If the secretary of the meeting is to be appointed by the meeting, use Form S–11B.

4. Scrutineers: appointment of scrutineers:

   (a) "If the meeting has no objection, I appoint Mr. T. and Mr. U as scrutineers to assist the Chair in the counting of votes (and proxies)."

   (b) If scrutineers are to be appointed by the meeting, use Form S–11C.

---

[13] *In smaller societies and at round-table style meetings, some of the opening formalities may be dispensed with (particularly the introduction of the officers).* There is no point in introducing the Chair and the secretary if everyone present knows them, nor is there any need to give a report on attendance when proxies are not permitted and all members are in sight of one another.

5. Proof of mailing notice (Form S–7):

    (a) "The notice calling the meeting was mailed to all the members of record (and others to whom notice is required to be sent) in accordance with the bylaws. A declaration to that effect is on file here for your perusal."

    (b) "Additional copies of the notice are available here if wanted."

6. Report on attendance (including proxies, if authorized):

    (a) "The scrutineers (*or* the secretary) reports on the attendance as follows:

    Members attending in person: . . . members.

    Acceptable proxies representing: . . . members.

    TOTAL in person and by proxy . . . members".

    (If the report is not ready, it may be read later).

    (b) "The Chair is advised that there is a quorum present, although the report on attendance is not yet ready. In the meantime, we will proceed with the meeting."

    (c) If the Chair does not adopt the secretary's (*or* the scrutineers') report on attendance: "The Chair has perused the attendance list and all the proxies questioned by the scrutineers, and declares that the attendance at this meeting is as follows: (*read the report as in 6(a) above*) There is a quorum present."

7. Verification of minutes of previous meeting (if required under the bylaws): see ¶ 3025, Verification of Minutes, page 160. "The minutes of the previous meeting of the society are available for perusal. Unless someone wishes them read, the Chair will entertain a motion to take the minutes as read and verified."

FORM S–16

Agenda for Board Meeting

[NAME OF SOCIETY]

AGENDA

for

Meeting of the board held ....

1. Chair calls meeting to order.

2. Secretary proves service of notice.

3. If quorum present, Chair declares meeting duly constituted.

4. Secretary reads minutes of last meeting. Chair asks for errors or omissions. Motion to verify. Discussion and vote. Chair declares result.

5. Business arising from the minutes.

6. Reports of officers and committees.

7. New business.

8. Motion to conclude.

FORM S–17

Ballot on Motion
[NAME OF SOCIETY]

Annual Meeting of Members held on [*date*]

BALLOT ON Motion No. [.....]

(A motion to ....)

I cast my vote   FOR [.....]   AGAINST [.....]

....

(Signature of person voting)

FORM S–18

Ballot on Motion (Proxies)
[NAME OF SOCIETY]

Annual Meeting of Members held on [*date*]

BALLOT ON Motion No. [.....]

(A motion to ....)

I cast my vote   FOR [.....]   AGAINST [.....]

I also cast proxy votes on behalf of the members who appointed me proxyholder for this purpose as per list annexed which has been verified by the scrutineers.

.... proxy votes verified

....

....

(Scrutineers)   *(Signature of person voting)*

FORM S–19

Ballot on Election of Directors

Annual Meeting of Members held on [*date*]

BALLOT ON ELECTION OF DIRECTORS

I cast my votes for the election of

1. A   B .... [...........]
2. C   D .... [...........]
3. E   F .... [...........]
4. G   H .... [...........]
5. I   J .... [...........]
6. K   L .... [...........]
7. M   N .... [...........]

....

(Signature of person voting)

FORM S–20

Ballot on Election of Directors (Proxies)

Annual Meeting of Members held on [*date*]
BALLOT ON ELECTION OF DIRECTORS

Nominees:

I cast my votes FOR			I cast my proxy votes FOR	
1. A	B...	[............]	....	[............]
2. C	D...	[............]	....	[............]
3. E	F...	[............]	....	[............]
4. G	H...	[............]	....	[............]
5. I	J...	[............]	....	[............]
6. K	L...	[............]	....	[............]
7. M	N...	[............]	....	[............]

The proxy votes are cast on behalf of the members who appointed me proxyholder for this purpose as per list annexed which has been verified by the scrutineers.

.... proxy votes verified

....

....
(Scrutineers)   *(Signature of person voting)*

FORM S–21

Ballot on Election of Officers and Directors (Direct Organization)[14]

Annual Meeting of Members held on [*date*]
BALLOT ON ELECTION OF OFFICERS AND DIRECTORS

PRESIDENT
Nominees: I cast my votes FOR[15]

1. A	B..	[............]
2. C	D..	[............]
3. E	F..	[............]
4. G	H..	[............]

The candidate with the second highest vote becomes vice-president.[16]

TREASURER
Nominees: I cast my votes FOR

1. A	B..	[............]
2. C	D..	[............]
3. E	F..	[............]

[14] This form must be modified to conform with the Society's constitution and practices.

[15] If proxies are authorized, modify according to Form S–20.

[16] or as the constitution provides.

DIRECTORS

Nominees: I cast my votes FOR

   1. A   B .... [...........]

   2. C   D .... [...........]

   3. E   F .... [...........]

   4. G   H .... [...........]

   5. I   J .... [...........]

   6. K   L .... [...........]

   7. M   N .... [...........]

Members may vote for any number up to five.[17]

The proxy votes are cast on behalf of the members who appointed me proxyholder for this purpose as per list annexed which has been verified by the scrutineers.

.... proxy votes verified

....

....

                   (Scrutineers)   ....

                                                       (Signature of person voting)

FORM S–22

Scrutineers' Report on Attendance
[NAME OF SOCIETY]
Meeting of Members held on *[date]*
SCRUTINEERS' REPORT ON ATTENDANCE

PRESENT IN PERSON

.... members (as per Exhibit "A" hereto)

REPRESENTED BY PROXY

According to proxies filed:

No. of members ....represented by ....

No. of members ....represented by ....

No. of members ....represented by ....

No. of members ....represented by ....

                                    Represented by proxy ....

                     TOTAL in person and by proxy ....

In addition to the proxies referred to above, there are proxies (as per Exhibit "B" hereto) which are, in our opinion, unacceptable, and we recommend that they be rejected.

The attendance in person and by proxy has been checked by us against the membership list.

DATED ....

                                        ....

                                                (Scrutineer)

                                        ....

                                                (Scrutineer)

---

[17] *supra* footnote 19.

FORM S–23

Scrutineers' Report on Motion
[NAME OF SOCIETY]

Meeting of Members held on [*date*]

SCRUTINEERS' REPORT ON MOTION NO. [.....] to ....

We, the undersigned scrutineers, report on the balloting on this motion as follows:

For the motion
  In person   ....
  By proxy   ....
  Total FOR   _____

Against the motion
  In person   ....
  By proxy   ....
  Total AGAINST   _____

Total votes cast   _____

....
    (*Scrutineer*)   (*Scrutineer*)

FORM S–24

Scrutineers' Report on Election of Directors
[NAME OF SOCIETY]

SCRUTINEERS' REPORT ON ELECTION OF DIRECTORS

[*Date*]

	Candidates	Votes
1.	....	....
2.	....	....
3.	....	....
4.	....	....
5.	....	....
6.	....	....
7.	....	....

....
    (*Scrutineer*)   (*Scrutineer*)

FORM S–25

Scrutineers' Report on Election of Directors (Proxies)

[NAME OF SOCIETY]

SCRUTINEERS' REPORT ON ELECTION OF DIRECTORS

We, the undersigned scrutineers, report on the balloting on the election of directors as follows:

Candidates	Votes Allowed	Disallowed
1.	....	....
2.	....	....
3.	....	....
4.	....	....
5.	....	....
6.	....	....
7.	....	....

The disallowed votes are based upon proxies which were disallowed by the Chair for the following reasons:

....

....

....

In addition and not counted were .... ballots which in our opinion are defective because:

- too many candidates listed   ....
- signature indecipherable   ....
- other defects   ....

DATED ....

          (*Scrutineer*)

          ....

          (*Scrutineer*)

FORM S–26

Scrutineers' Report on Election of Officers
(Direct Organization)

[NAME OF SOCIETY]

SCRUTINEERS' REPORT ON ELECTION OF OFFICERS

We, the undersigned scrutineers, report on the balloting on the election of officers as follows:

Candidates	Votes Allowed	Disallowed
1.	....	....
2.	....	....
3.	....	....
4.	....	....
5.	....	....
6.	....	....
7.	....	....

The disallowed votes are based upon proxies which were disallowed by the Chair for the following reasons:

....

....

....

In addition and not counted were .... ballots which in our opinion are defective because:

- too many candidates listed   ....
- signature indecipherable   ....
- other defects   ....

DATED ....

                                          (Scrutineer)

                       ....

                                            (Scrutineer)

FORM S–27

Minutes of Annual Meeting (Indirect Organization)

MINUTES of the annual meeting of members of *[name of Society]* held at *[place]* on *[date]* at *[time].*

1. Opening the meeting:

Mr. C, the president of the Society, called the meeting to order and acted as Chair, and Mr. S, secretary of the Society, acted as secretary of the meeting.[18] The Chair appointed Mr. T and Mr. U scrutineers.[19]

---

[18] For variations, see Form S–27A.

[19] For variations, see Form S–27B.

2. Notice of meeting:

> The notice calling this annual meeting of members[20] was sent to all members in good standing on [*date*] in accordance with the bylaws [*or* constitution] of the Society as evidenced by the declaration of Mr. .... annexed to these minutes as Annex "A".

3. Attendance:

> The scrutineers reported that there were [.....] members in good standing present in person and there were [.....] members in good standing represented by proxy, of which [.....] were in favour of Mr. C and [.....] in favour of W.A. The Chair adopted the report of the scrutineers and declared accordingly. The scrutineers' report on attendance is annexed to these minutes as Annex "B".

4. Constitution of meeting:

> The Chair declared that notice of this meeting had been duly given to all members of the Society in good standing in accordance with the bylaws [*or* constitution] of the Society, that there was a quorum present, and that the meeting was duly constituted for the transaction of business.

5. Approval of agenda:

> The agenda was circulated to the meeting [*or*, distributed before the meeting]. It was moved, seconded, and unanimously carried that the agenda as submitted be approved. [*Add, if applicable*: with the following changes (*set out changes to the proposed agenda*).]

6. Minutes of previous meeting:

> The Chair advised the meeting that the minutes of the last meeting of members were available for perusal by the members and would be read if any member so desired.[21] No such request was made, and upon motion duly made by Mr. L, seconded by Mr. M, and unanimously carried, it was
>
> > "Resolved, That the minutes of the annual meeting of members held on [*date*] be taken as read and verified."

7. Report of the board of directors:

> The president reported on the activities of the Society during the past year. [*Summarize the report. If the report is in writing, attach it to the minutes.*]

8. Report of the treasurer (financial statement):

> The treasurer presented to the meeting the financial statement and auditors' report for the year ended [*date*]. The following motion was made by Mr. G and seconded by Mr. H:
>
> > "Resolved, That the financial statement for the year ended [*date*] (including the balance sheet and accompanying statements, together with the auditors' report thereon) and all the transactions reflected thereby, be approved."
>
> A poll was taken and the Chair declared the resolution duly carried by a vote of ...... votes FOR and .... votes AGAINST. The scrutineers' report is annexed to these minutes as Schedule "C".

---

[20] For variations, see Form S–27C.

[21] Unless required by the constitution or the bylaws, reading or verifying the minutes of previous meetings is not necessary. For variations, see Form S–27D.

9. Budget for current year:

   The treasurer presented the budget for the current year. A copy of the budget is annexed to these minutes as Exhibit "D".

10. Reports of committees:

   The Chair of the .... committee presented the report of that committee. [*Summarize the report. If the report is in writing, attach it to the minutes.*]

11. Election of directors:

   The Chair called for nominations for directors of the Society, and the following persons were nominated: ....

   ....

   ....

   On motion duly made, seconded, and unanimously carried, nominations were closed.[22]

   Only five persons having been nominated and no member having demanded a ballot,[23] the Chair declared [*names*] to be duly elected directors of the Society, to hold office until their successors are duly elected or appointed.

12. Appointment of auditors:

   On motion duly made by Mr. P and seconded by Mr. Q and unanimously carried, it was

   "Resolved, That Messrs. .... be appointed auditors of the Society, to hold office until the next annual meeting or until their successors are duly appointed, and the board of directors be authorized to fix the remuneration of the auditors." [*Add, if indicated:* on the basis of that presently paid.]"

13. Conclusion:

   On motion duly made by Mr. M, seconded by Mr. N, and unanimously carried, the meeting was concluded.

   ....
          (*Chair*)   (*Secretary*)

   VERIFIED at the meeting of members held ....

   ....
          (*Chair*)

FORM S–27A — Variations: Chair and Secretary

1. Vice-President chairs meeting:

   In the absence [*or* refusal] of the president, Mr. D, the vice-president, acted as Chair of the meeting.

2. Chair is elected by resolution:

   On motion duly made by Mr. M, seconded by Mr. N, and unanimously carried, it was

   "Resolved, That Mr. C be elected Chair of the meeting. Mr. C acted as Chair."

------

[22] For variations, see Form S–27E.

[23] For variations, see Form S–27F.

3. Chair is elected by ballot:

> Mr. C and Mr. D were nominated for Chair of the meeting. A poll was taken, Mr. C was declared elected, and he acted as Chair of the meeting.

4. Chair and secretary are elected by resolution:

> On motion duly made by Mr. M, seconded by Mr. N, and unanimously carried, it was
>
> > "Resolved, That Mr. C be elected Chair, and Mr. S be secretary of the meeting."

5. Secretary is appointed by resolution:

> On motion duly made by Mr. M, seconded by Mr. N, and unanimously carried, it was
>
> > "Resolved, That Mr. S be and is hereby appointed secretary of the meeting."

FORM S–27B — Variation: Scrutineers

> On motion duly made, seconded, and unanimously carried, it was
>
> > "Resolved, That Mr. T and Mr. V are hereby appointed scrutineers to assist the Chair in counting attendance, proxies, and ballots."

FORM S–27C — Variation: Notice Mailed

> The Chair declared that notice of this meeting having been mailed to each member in accordance with the bylaws of the Society and a quorum being present, the meeting was duly constituted for the transaction of business.

FORM S–27D — Variation: If the Report on Attendance was not Ready

> The Chair stated that the report on attendance was not ready. He declared that there was a quorum present and that the meeting was duly constituted for the transaction of business. Subsequently, the scrutineers' report on attendance was submitted, and the Chair adopted the report and declared the attendance at the meeting to be as follows:

> > Present in person ....
> >
> > Represented by proxy in favour of..
> >
> > Represented by proxy in favour of..

> The scrutineers' report was directed to be annexed to the minutes of the meeting, and the proxies were directed to be filed with the records of the Society.

FORM S–27E — Variation: If Minutes Taken as Read

> On motion duly made, seconded, and unanimously carried, it was
>
> > "Resolved, That the minutes of the previous meeting of members held on .... be taken as read and verified."

FORM S–27F — Variations: Election by Acclamation

1. Nominations closed by resolution:

> The Chair called for further nominations and none were offered. On motion duly made, seconded, and unanimously carried, it was
>
> > "Resolved, That nominations be closed."

2. Nominations. Election by ballot:

The Chair called for further nominations. None were offered and the Chair declared nominations closed. Upon motion duly made by Mr. M, seconded by Mr. N, and unanimously carried, it was

"Resolved, That only five persons having been nominated as directors of the Society, and the Chair having declared nominations closed, the secretary be directed to cast a single ballot for the election of those nominated as directors."

The secretary cast a ballot as directed and the Chair thereupon declared ....
.... to be duly elected directors of the Society, to hold office until their successors are duly elected or appointed.

FORM S–28

Minutes of Annual Meeting (Direct Organization)

MINUTES of the annual meeting of members of [*name of Society*]
held at [*place*] on [*date*] at [*time*].

1. Opening the meeting:

Mr. C, the president of the Society, called the meeting to order and acted as Chair of the meeting, and Mr. S, secretary of the Society, acted as secretary of the meeting. On motion duly made, seconded, and unanimously carried, Mr. T and Mr. U were appointed scrutineers.

2. Notice of meeting:

The notice calling this meeting of the Society was sent to all members in good standing on [*date*] in accordance with the bylaws [*or* articles] of the Society as evidenced by the declaration of Mr. .... The declaration is annexed to these minutes as Schedule "A".

3. Attendance:

The Chair requested that all members present give their names to and deposit all proxies with the scrutineers. [*If proxies are required to be deposited before the meeting (see Rule 14.1, Formal Requirements, page 70), omit reference to them.*]

The scrutineers reported that there were [.....] members in good standing present in person and there were [.....] members in good standing represented by proxy, making a grand total of [.....] members represented in person and by proxy.

The Chair examined the proxies and declared that he was not adopting the scrutineers' report on attendance. The Chair declared that there were [.....] members present in person and [.....] members represented by proxy, making a total of [.....] members represented in person and by proxy. The scrutineers' report on attendance is annexed to these minutes as Schedule "B".

4. Constitution of meeting:

The Chair declared that notice of this meeting had been duly given to all members of the Society in accordance with the bylaws [*or* constitution] of the Society, that there was a quorum present, and that the meeting was duly constituted for the transaction of business.

231

5. Approval of agenda:

The agenda was circulated to the meeting [*or*, distributed before the meeting]. It was moved, seconded, and unanimously carried that the agenda as submitted be approved. [*Add, if applicable:* with the following changes (*set out changes to the proposed agenda*).]

6. Minutes of previous meeting:

The Chair advised the meeting that the minutes of the previous meeting of members were available for perusal by the members and would be read if any member so desired. No such request was made, and upon motion duly made by Mr. L, seconded by Mr. M, and unanimously carried, it was

"Resolved, That the minutes of the annual meeting of members held on [*date*] be taken as read and verified."

7. Report of the board of directors:

The treasurer reported on the activities of the Society during the past year. [*Summarize the report. If the report is in writing, attach it to the minutes.*]

8. Report of the treasurer (financial statement):

The treasurer presented to the meeting the financial statement and auditors' report for the year ended [*date*]. The following motion was made by Mr. G and seconded by Mr. H:

"Resolved, That the financial statement for the year ended [*date*] (including the balance sheet and accompanying statements, together with the auditors' report thereon) and all the transactions reflected thereby, be approved."

A poll was taken and the Chair declared the resolution duly carried by a vote of .... votes FOR and .... votes AGAINST. The scrutineers' report is annexed to these minutes as Schedule "C".

9. Budget for current year:

The treasurer presented the budget for the current year. A copy of the budget is annexed to these minutes as Exhibit "D".

10. Reports of committees:

The Chair of the .... committee presented the report of that committee. [*Summarize the report. If the report is in writing, attach it to the minutes.*]

11. Election of directors:

The Chair declared the meeting open for the election of directors, and called for nominations. The following were nominated as directors: A, B, C, D, E, F, and G.

On motion duly made, seconded, and unanimously carried, nominations were closed.

Since more than the required number of directors were nominated, the Chair directed that a poll be taken. The secretary distributed ballots and instructed the members on the use of the ballots. The scrutineers collected the ballots and retired to complete the count. The meeting was recessed for thirty minutes.

The scrutineers reported to the Chair on the ballot for the election of directors as follows:

A .... votes

B .... votes

C .... votes

D .... votes

E .... votes

F .... votes

G .... votes

The Chair examined the ballots and the scrutineers' report and declared that he/she was not adopting the scrutineers' report. The Chair declared the result of the poll as follows:

A .... votes

B .... votes

C .... votes

D .... votes

E .... votes

F .... votes

G .... votes

and declared A, C, D, E, and G duly elected directors of the Society, to hold office until their successors are duly elected or appointed.

12. Election of officers:

The Chair declared the meeting open for the election of officers, and called for nominations for president and vice-president. The following persons were nominated for president: A, B, and C. The following persons were nominated for vice-president: D and E.

On motion duly made, seconded, and unanimously carried, nominations were closed.

Since the elections of the president and the vice-president were both contested, the Chair directed that a poll be taken. The secretary distributed ballots and instructed the members on the use of the ballots. The scrutineers collected the ballots and retired to complete the count. The meeting was recessed for ten minutes.

The scrutineers reported to the Chair on the ballot for the election of the president and vice-president as follows:

PRESIDENT	A	_____ votes
	B	_____ votes
	C	_____ votes
VICE-PRESIDENT	A	_____ votes
	B	_____ votes

The Chair examined the ballots and the scrutineers' report and adopted the scrutineers' report. The Chair then declared A elected as President and D as Vice-President of the Society, to hold office until their successors are duly elected or appointed.

13. Appointment of auditors:

The Chair declared the meeting open for the appointment of auditors.

The following resolution was duly moved by Mr. S, seconded by Mr. T:

"Resolved, That Messrs. Bee and Bee are appointed auditors of the Society, to hold office until the next annual meeting or until their successors are duly appointed, and the board of directors be authorized to fix the remuneration of the auditors. [*Add, if indicated:* on the basis of that presently paid.]"[24]

On motion duly made by Mr. M, seconded by Mr. N, and unanimously carried, the meeting was concluded.

....

(*Chair*)   (*Secretary*)

VERIFIED at the meeting of   held ....

....

(*Chair*)

FORM S–29

Minutes of Board Meeting

MINUTES of a meeting of the board of directors of [*name of Society*] held at [*place*] on [*date*] at [*time*].

PRESENT .... being all [*or a quorum*] of the directors of the Society [and .... by invitation of the board].

A. Formalities

Mr. A, president of the Society, acted as Chair of the meeting, and Mr. B, secretary of the Society, acted as secretary of the meeting. (For variations, see Form S–27A.)

Notice convening the meeting having been sent to all the directors in accordance with the bylaws of the Society, and a quorum being present, the Chair declared the meeting duly constituted for the transaction of business.

B. Minutes of Previous Meeting

Minutes of the previous meeting of the board were read by the secretary and, on motion duly made, seconded, and unanimously carried, it was

Resolved, That the minutes of the previous meeting held on [*date*] be taken as read and verified." (For variations, see Form S–29A.)

C. Business of the Meeting

[*Set out the business conducted at the meeting.*] (See sample forms S–29B and S–29C.)

---

[24] If the motion is defeated, another motion may be moved (*Rule 24.7, Appointments, page 133*).

Forms for Society Meetings

D. Conclusion

There being no further business, the meeting was concluded.

....
(*Chair*)   (*Secretary*)

FORM S–29A — Variations: Minutes Taken as Read

(i) *On Motion*

On motion duly made, seconded, and unanimously carried, it was

"Resolved, That the minutes of the previous meeting of the board held on [*date*], as mailed to every director, be taken as read and verified."

(ii) *Without Motion*

Minutes of the previous meeting of the board held on [*date*], copies of which had been mailed to each director, were taken as read and were verified.

FORM S–29B — Resolution to Call Annual Meeting

Calling of Annual Meeting:

On motion duly made by Mr. M, seconded by Mr. N, and unanimously carried, it was

1. "Resolved, That an annual meeting of the members of the Society be held as soon as convenient, and that the secretary be authorized and directed to do all things necessary or desirable for the purpose of convening such a meeting";

2. "Resolved, That the draft form of annual report to the members, the notice of meeting, and proxyform in favour of D, or failing him, E, as presented to the meeting, be approved, the president having authority on the advice of the Society's solicitor to make such changes therein as in his opinion are necessary or desirable."

FORM S–29C — Resolution to Call General Meeting

Calling of General Meeting:

On motion duly made, seconded, and unanimously carried, it was

1. "Resolved, That a general meeting of the [*name of Society*] be held as soon as convenient for the purpose of .... , and that the secretary be authorized and directed to do all things necessary or desirable for the purpose of convening such a meeting";

2. "Resolved, That the draft form of notice of meeting and proxyform in favour of D, or failing him, E, as presented to the meeting, be approved, the president having authority on the advice of the Society's solicitor, to make such changes therein as in his opinion are necessary or desirable."

235

FORM S–30

Minutes of Board Meeting Following Annual Meeting

MINUTES of a meeting of the board of directors of [*name of Society*] held at [*place*] on [*date*] at [*time*].

PRESENT .... being all [*or* a quorum] of the directors of the Society [and .... by invitation of the board].

1. Chair and secretary:

   By motion duly made, seconded, and unanimously carried, Mr. A acted as Chair of the meeting and Mr. B as secretary of the meeting.

2. Constitution of meeting:

   The Chair declared that all [*or* a quorum] of the directors having waived notice of the meeting and that a quorum of directors being present, the meeting was duly constituted.[25]

3. Minutes of previous meeting:

   The minutes of the previous meeting of the board were read by the secretary and, on motion duly made, seconded, and unanimously carried, it was

   "Resolved, That the minutes of the previous meeting of the board held on [*date*] be verified."[26]

4. Election of officers:

   On motion duly made, seconded, and unanimously carried, it was

   "Resolved, That the following persons be elected or appointed officers of the company to hold the office referred to opposite their respective names for the ensuing year or until their successors are duly elected or appointed":

President:	A ....
Vice-President:	B ....
Secretary:	C ....
Treasurer:	D ....

5. Conclusion of meeting:

   There being no further business, the meeting was concluded.

....
         (*Chair*)   (*Secretary*)

---

[25] Some constitutions provide that no notice is required for routine business conducted by the board immediately after an annual meeting, provided that all directors are present or that those absent have waived notice of the meeting.

In such case, use the following wording under the heading "Constitution of Meeting":

"This being the first meeting of the board elected at the annual meeting, held immediately after the annual meeting, and all directors being present [*or* a quorum of directors being present and those absent having waived notice of the meeting], the Chair declared that the meeting was duly constituted."

[26] For variation, see Form S–27E.

We, the undersigned, verify the above minutes and acknowledge having waived notice of the meeting. We approve all the resolutions passed and business transacted thereat.

....

....

....

FORM S–31

Minutes of Meetings (Short Form)

MINUTES of a meeting of members (board of directors/ .... committee) held [*date and time*].

1. Chair:

2. Secretary:

3. Present: (*Names of members/directors/committee members*)

4. Guests: (*if any*)

5. Regrets: (*Reasons for absence may be included*)

6. Resolutions: (*May include defeated motions*)

7. Reports: (*Business, financial, etc.*)

8. Other: (*Talks, lectures, demonstrations, etc.*)

9. Next meeting:

....

           (*Chair*)   (*Secretary*)

Appendix B

Condominium Forms

NOTE: For Chair's agenda, see Appendix A, Form S-11, page 210.

FORM CO–1

Notice of Annual Meeting

MUNICIPALITY CONDOMINIUM CORPORATION NO. XX

NOTICE OF ANNUAL MEETING OF OWNERS

NOTICE IS HEREBY GIVEN that the Annual Meeting of the Owners of [*full name of the condominium corporation*] will be held on [*date*] in the Party Room [*address*] at 8 p.m. for the purposes outlined in the annexed agenda.

Registration will commence at 7:30 p.m. so that the meeting will start on time.

If you will not be attending, please complete the annexed Proxyform and hand it to any director or officer or the person whom you have appointed to act as your proxy.

By order of the board

[*or as the case may be*]

....
(*Signature*)

FORM CO–2

Notice of Special Meeting

MUNICIPALITY CONDOMINIUM CORPORATION NO. XX

NOTICE OF SPECIAL MEETING OF OWNERS

NOTICE IS HEREBY GIVEN that a Special Meeting of the Owners of [*full name of condominium corporation*] will be held on [*date*] in the Party Room [*address*] at 8 p.m. for the purpose of:

— considering a motion to remove ABC as a director of the Corporation before the expiration of his term of office, and

— electing a qualified person to act as a director for the remainder of the term, *or*

— for the following purposes: [*set out the purposes of the meeting*].

Registration will commence at 7:30 p.m. so that the meeting will start on time.

If you will not be attending, please complete the annexed Proxyform and hand it to any director or officer or the person whom you have appointed to act as your proxy.

By order of the board

[*or as the case may be*]

....
(*Signature*)

240

Condominium Forms

(*Add, where indicated:* NOTE: Except where, under the Act or the bylaws of the condominium corporation, a unanimous vote of all owners is required, an owner is not entitled to vote at a meeting if any contributions payable in respect of his/her unit are in arrears for more than thirty days prior to the meeting.)

FORM CO–3

Requisition for Meeting of Owners

MUNICIPALITY CONDOMINIUM CORPORATION NO. XX

TO: Municipality Condominium Corporation No. xx

And to the Board of Directors thereof:

TAKE NOTICE that the undersigned owners of units of .... [*full name of the condominium corporation*] pursuant to Section ..... of the *Condominium Act* ..... [*cite Act*] and amendments thereto HEREBY REQUIRE that a Special (*or* Annual) Meeting of the Owners of .... [*full name of the condominium corporation*] be called and held within the time required by the Act for the following purposes:

1. To consider and vote upon a motion to remove all the directors [*or, the names of specific directors*] before the expiration of his/their term/s of office, and

2. To elect a person qualified to be a director for each position vacated, for the remainder of the term of each director removed, *or*

3. [*Set out clearly the purposes for which it is desired to requisition the meeting.*]

Suite No. .... Name of Owner/s .... Signatures ....

FORM CO–4

Proxyform for Annual Meeting — Short Form

MUNICIPALITY CONDOMINIUM CORPORATION NO. XX

I, the undersigned owner of Suite No. .... of Municipality Condominium No. XX, HEREBY APPOINT .... [*name of proxyholder*] as my/our proxy to attend and act for me/us at the Annual Meeting of the Owners of .... [*full name of the condominium corporation*] to be held on .... [*date*] at .... [*time*] and all adjournments thereof.

The said proxyholder shall act to the same extent and with the same power as I/we could if I/we were present at the said meeting.

Dated this .... day of .... 19....

....
(*Signature(s) of Owner(s)*)

241

FORM CO–5

Proxyform for Annual Meeting

MUNICIPALITY CONDOMINIUM CORPORATION NO. XX

THE UNDERSIGNED, being the owner(s)(or mortgagee(s)) of the suite designated below of the ..... [*full name of the condominium corporation*] HEREBY APPOINTS ..... [*name of proxyholder*] or, ... whom failing, the Secretary of the Corporation, or, whom failing, the President of the Corporation, as my/our proxy to attend and act for me/us at the Annual Meeting of the Owners of ..... [*full name of the condominium corporation*] (and all adjournments thereof) to be held on .... [*date*] .... at .... [*time*].

The said proxyholder shall act to the same extent and with the same power as we could if we were present at the said meeting.

Dated this .... day of .... 19....

Suite No. ....

....
(*Signature(s) of Owner(s)*)

....
(*Owners or Mortgagees*)

FORM CO–6

Proxyform for Special Meeting

MUNICIPALITY CONDOMINIUM CORPORATION NO. XX

THE UNDERSIGNED, being the owner(s) (or mortgagee(s)) of the suite designated below of the .... [*full name of the condominium corporation*] HEREBY APPOINT ...... [*name of proxyholder*] or, ... whom failing, the Secretary of the Corporation, or, whom failing, the President of the Corporation, as proxy of the undersigned to attend and act for me/us at the Annual Meeting of the Owners of .... [*full name of the condominium corporation*] (and all adjournments thereof) to be held on ...... [*date*] .... at ...... [*time*].

The said proxyholder shall act to the same extent and with the same power as we could if we were present at the said meeting.

Dated this .... day of .... 19....

Suite No. ....

....
(*Signature(s) of Owner(s)*)

....
(*Owners or Mortgagees*)

FORM CO–7

Proxyform for Special Meeting with Instructions

MUNICIPALITY CONDOMINIUM CORPORATION NO. XX

THE UNDERSIGNED, being the owner(s) (mortgagee(s)) of the suite designated below of the ..... [*full name of the condominium corporation*] HEREBY APPOINTS ..... [*name of proxyholder*] or, ... whom failing, the Secretary of the Corporation, or, whom failing, the President of the Corporation, as proxy of the undersigned to attend and act at the Annual Meeting of the Owners of the condominium corporation (and all adjournments thereof) to be held on .... [*date*] .... at .... [*time*].

The said proxyholder shall vote in favour of motions to ...... against motions to ..... and on all other business, to act to the same extent and with the same power as the undersigned could if present at the said meeting.

Dated this .... day of .... 19....

Suite No. ....

....
(*Signatures of Owners*)

....
(*Owners or Mortgagees*)

NOTE: For Chair's agendas, see Forms S–11, S–13, and S–15.

FORM CO–8

Agenda for Annual Meeting of Owners

(See also Appendix A, Form S–11, Chair's Agenda, page 210)

1. Opening the meeting; registration of members.

2. Chair: introduction or appointment.

3. Secretary: introduction or designation.

4. Scrutineers: appointment.

5. Introduction of guests.

6. Proof of mailing or delivery of notice of meeting.

7. Report on attendance (including proxies, if authorized).

8. Verification of minutes of previous annual meeting (if required).

9. Approval of agenda: business arising from the minutes.

10. Report of the Board of Directors and/or the manager (Annual Report).

11. Report of the Treasurer, financial statement.

12. Budget for the current year.

13. Reports of standing committees.

14. Reports of special committees.

15. Election of directors: (as required)

    - 2 directors for a one-year term,
    - 1 director for a two-year term, and
    - 1 director for a three-year term.

16. Appointment of auditors.

17. New business for which due notice has been given.

18. New business for which prior notice is not required.

19. Conclusion of meeting.

Appendix C

Co-Operative Forms

NOTE: Notice of Meetings of the Board and Minutes of Meetings of the Board, as well as other forms, may be adapted from Appendix A, Forms for Society Meetings, page 203.

FORM CU–1

Waiver of Notice of Board Meeting

NAME CO-OPERATIVE INC.

The undersigned directors of Name Co-Operative Inc. hereby waive notice of a meeting of the board of directors of the co-operative to be held at [*address*] on [*date*] at [*time*].

Dated the .... day of .... 19....

....
(*Signatures*)

FORM CU–2

Waiver of Notice of Meeting of Members

NAME CO-OPERATIVE INC.

The undersigned members of Name Co-Operative Inc. hereby waive notice of a special meeting of the members of the co-operative to be held at [*address*] on [*date*] at [*time*].

Dated the .... day of .... 19....

....
(*Signatures*)

FORM CU–3

Consent to Act as a Director

CONSENT TO ACT AS A DIRECTOR

TO: Name Co-Operative Inc.

I DECLARE that I am a Canadian citizen, at least 18 years old, ordinarily resident in Canada, not mentally incompetent, and not an undischarged bankrupt. If my residence status changes, I agree to immediately notify the Co-operative.

I HEREBY CONSENT to act as a director of the Co-operative. I further consent to the holding of meetings of the board of directors by means of any communication medium that permits all participating persons to speak to and hear each other simultaneously.

THIS CONSENT shall remain in effect as long as I am a director or until I revoke it in writing.

Dated the .... day of .... 19....

....
(*Signature*)

246

FORM CU–4

Notice of Annual Meeting

NOTICE OF THE (*16TH*) ANNUAL MEETING
OF NAME CO-OPERATIVE INC.

TO the members:

TAKE NOTICE that the (*16th*) annual meeting of the Co-operative will be held at [*full address*] on [*date*] at [*time*] [*local time*] for the purpose of:

- receiving and considering the report of the board on the business and affairs of the Co-operative and any other matters required by the rules;

- receiving and considering the balance sheet, general statement of income, and expenditures;

- electing a board of directors;

- appointing auditors; and

- transacting such other business as may be properly brought before the meeting.

(*Add, if indicated:* To consider, and if approved, pass, with or without amendment, the following as a special (*or, extraordinary*) resolution: (*the proposed resolution should be set out in full or annexed to the notice*))

Dated the .... day of .... 19....

By order of the board of directors

....
(*Secretary*)

Appendix D

Lists of Statutes

FEDERAL AND PROVINCIAL STATUTES
GOVERNING SOCIETIES

Federal

Canada Corporations Act, R.S.C. 1970, c. C-32

Alberta

Societies Act, R.S.A. 1980, c. S-18

British Columbia

Architects (Landscape) Act, R.S.B.C. 1979, c. 20

Society Act, R.S.B.C. 1979, c. 390

Manitoba

Corporations Act, R.S.M. 1987, c. C225

New Brunswick

Companies Act, R.S.N.B. 1973, c. C-13, s. 18

Newfoundland

Corporations Act, S.N. 1986, c. 12

Nova Scotia

Community Act, R.S.N.S. 1989, c. 80

Religious Congregations and Societies Act, R.S.N.S. 1989, c. 395

Societies Act, R.S.N.S. 1989, c. 435

Ontario

Agricultural and Horticultural Organizations Act, R.S.O. 1990, c. A.9

Athletics Control Act, R.S.O. 1990, c. A.34

Community Recreation Centres Act, R.S.O. 1990, c. C.22

Corporations Act, R.S.O. 1990, c. C.38, Part III

Municipal Act, R.S.O. 1990, c. M.45, s. 20–21

Religious Organizations' Lands Act, R.S.O. 1990, c. R.23

Trustee Act, R.S.O. 1990, c. T.23, s. 10(1)(*f*)

Prince Edward Island

Companies Act, R.S.P.E.I. 1988, c. C-14

Quebec

Companies Act, R.S.Q. 1977, c. C-38

Religious Corporations Act, R.S.Q. 1977, c. C-71

Saskatchewan

Agricultural Societies Act, R.S.S. 1978, c. A-15

Association of School Business Officials of Saskatchewan Act, R.S.S. 1978, c. A-31

Non-Profit Corporations Act, S.S. 1979, c. N-4.1

Yukon

Societies Act, S.Y. 1987, c. 32

PROVINCIAL STATUTES GOVERNING CONDOMINIUMS

Alberta

Condominium Property Act, R.S.A. 1980, c. C-22

British Columbia

Condominium Act, R.S.B.C. 1979, c. 61

Manitoba

Condominium Act, R.S.M. 1987, c. C170

New Brunswick

Condominium Property Act, R.S.N.B. 1973, c. C-16

Newfoundland

Condominium Act, R.S.N. 1970, c. 57

Nova Scotia

Condominium Act, R.S.N.S. 1989, c. 85

Ontario

Condominium Act, R.S.O. 1990, c. C.26

Prince Edward Island

Condominium Act, R.S.P.E.I. 1988, c. C-16

Saskatchewan

Condominium Property Act, R.S.S. 1978, c. C-26

Northwest Territories

Condominium Act, R.S.N.W.T. 1988, c. C-15

Yukon

Condominium Act, R.S.Y. 1986, c. 28

FEDERAL AND PROVINCIAL STATUTES
GOVERNING CO-OPERATIVES

Federal

Canada Cooperative Associations Act, R.S.C. 1985, c. C-40

Cooperative Credit Associations Act, R.S.C. 1985, c. C-41

Alberta

Co-operative Associations Act, R.S.A. 1980, c. C-24

British Columbia

Cooperative Association Act, R.S.B.C. 1979, c. 66

Manitoba

Cooperatives Act, R.S.M. 1987, c. C223

New Brunswick

Co-operative Associations Act, S.N.B. 1978, c. C-22.1

Newfoundland

Co-operative Societies Act, R.S.N. 1970, c. 65

Nova Scotia

Co-operative Associations Act, R.S.N.S. 1989, c. 98

Ontario

Co-operative Corporations Act, R.S.O. 1990, c. C.35

Prince Edward Island

Co-operative Associations Act, R.S.P.E.I. 1988, c. C-23

Quebec

Cooperatives Act, S.Q. 1982, c. 26

Saskatchewan

The Co-operatives Act, 1989, S.S. 1989-90, c. C-37.2

Northwest Territories

Co-operative Associations Act, R.S.N.W.T. 1988, c. C-19

Yukon

Cooperative Association Act, R.S.Y. 1986, c. 34

PROVINCIAL STATUTES GOVERNING CREDIT UNIONS

Alberta

Credit Union Act, S.A. 1989, c. C-31.1

British Columbia

Financial Institutions Act, S.B.C. 1989, c. 47

Credit Union Incorporation Act, S.B.C. 1989, c. 23

Manitoba

Credit Unions and Caisses Populaires Act, C.C.S.M., c. C301

New Brunswick

Credit Unions Act, S.N.B. 1977, c. C-32.1

Credit Union Federations Act, R.S.N.B. 1973, c. C-31

Newfoundland

Co-operative Societies Act, R.S.N. 1970, c. 65

Nova Scotia

Credit Union Act, R.S.N.S. 1989, c. 111

Ontario

Credit Unions and Caisses Populaires Act, R.S.O. 1990, c. C.44

Prince Edward Island

Credit Unions Act, R.S.P.E.I. 1988, c. C-29

Quebec

Savings and Credit Unions Act, S.Q. 1988, c. 64

Saskatchewan

Credit Union Act, 1985, S.S. 1984-85-86, c. C-45.1

Northwest Territories

Credit Union Act, R.S.N.W.T. 1988, c. C-23

INDEX

The main references in this index are to page numbers. However, for greater speed and clarity entries are also referenced by Rule number, paragraph number (¶), and Form number, where applicable.

Index

Mee

Mee

Mee 264

Index

Index

Sen

Index